"PROFOUND"

"HAUNTING"

"CHALLENGING"

"A profound, nourishing book which is absolutely essential to the understanding of our troubled times. Ernest Becker has plumbed the darkest aspects of our experience and given us the insight we most desperately need."

—Anaïs Nin

"[A] challenging book—a guide into the shadowy labyrinths of Everyman's psyche."

—*The Grand Rapids Press*

"An urgent essay that bears all the marks of a final philosophical raging against the dying of the light. . . . The beauty—and terror—of his final testament lies in his unsparing analysis of how men from time immemorial have sought scapegoats and victims in order to bolster their intimations of immortality . . . . "

—*Newsweek*

"A masterful study of man's struggle to transcend death through culture, and the evil which ensues . . . . an invaluable and haunting insight into the root of man's evil."

The Sunday Oklahoman

"This brilliant and challenging book, written as Becker lay dying, adds another bit of reason to balance destruction . . . . it is a work of felicity and the kind of erudition that makes Becker much more than the label of cultural anthropologist suggests . . . . It is, in the best sense of the words, both scientific and philosophical . . . . His contribution to the continuing dialogue is of the highest importance."

—Robert Kirsch, *The Los Angeles Times*

"This is one of those few books which will affect all your subsequent reading, and help shape your self-awareness."

—*The Providence Sunday Journal*

"Shuttling constantly among the individual, the culture and the cosmos, [Becker's] book is a synthesis of anthropology, Freud, Otto Rank, Norman O. Brown, and his own considerable fund of observation and formulation . . . . "

—Anatole Broyard, *The New York Times*

"BRILLIANT"
"EXTRAORDINARY"
"EXHILARATING"

"Becker has carried forward his **brilliant synthesis of post-Freudian thought** . . . . Writing with remarkable simplicity and insight . . . **has a haunting coherence and a built-in challenge** to the serious reader seeking a solution to man's irrational destructiveness."
—*Publisher's Weekly*

"This extraordinary and wide-ranging book . . . should stimulate the search for philosophical and psychological systems that are more realistic about the human condition."
—Margaret Manning, *The Boston Sunday Globe*

"A brilliant generalist with a neo-Freudian perspective, Becker surveys anthropology, existential philosophy and psychoanalysis for the foundations of a science of society . . . . His work will be a great help to the many generalists now working on a post-Freudian, post-Marxian synthesis."
—*The Detroit Free Press*

"**An exploration of the natural history of evil** . . . . gather[s] the best insights into the human condition, fashioning them into a general theory of man . . . . Becker began as a cultural anthropologist, but he ended as a formidable polymath . . . . *Escape From Evil* is a profound final testament . . . . an appropriate culmination of his career . . . ."
—*The Chronicle of Higher Education Review*

"**The author's presence—high on ideas, bold and disorderly, outrageous and appreciative, always in search—has an exhilarating effect** . . . . Becker's tone is . . . urgent and animated—he is still there arguing, doubting, debating with himself, despairing, looking for and rarely finding avenues of human hope. Again he displays his extraordinary synthetic gift as he moves freely, even dazzlingly, not only from Freud to Marx and from Rank to Brown, but from Rousseau to Hobbes, Huizinga, Mumford, Hugh Duncan and Kenneth Burke . . . . Becker's work should give powerful impetus to the development of a depth psychology appropriate to our condition and our history, but with significance beyond the historical moment . . . . Any future social theory will owe much to Becker, as does contemporary psychological thought . . . . The power of the work prevails."
—Robert Jay Lifton, *The New York Times Book Review*

ESCAPE
FROM
EVIL

Ernest Becker

THE FREE PRESS

New York   London   Toronto   Sydney   Singapore

THE FREE PRESS
A Division of Simon & Schuster Inc.
1230 Avenue of the Americas
New York, NY 10020

Copyright © 1975 by Marie Becker

Manufactured in the United States of America

20 19 18 17 16 15

Library of Congress Catalog Card Number: 75–12059

ISBN-13: 978-0-02902-450-8
ISBN-10: 0-02902-450-1

*In memory of Otto Rank, whose thought
may well prove to be the rarest gift of Freud's
disciples to the world.*

There is no doubt that healthy-mindedness is inadequate as a philosophical doctrine, because the evil facts which it positively refuses to account for are a genuine portion of reality; and they may after all be the best key to life's significance, and possibly the only openers of our eyes to the deepest levels of truth.

William James[1]

*If a way to the better there be, it lies in
taking a full look at the worst.*
Thomas Hardy

Why, if it's possible to spend this span
of existence as laurel, a little darker than all
other greens, with little waves on every
leaf-edge (like the smile of a breeze), why, then,
must we be human and, shunning destiny,
long for it? . . .
                    Oh, not because happiness,
that over-hasty profit of loss impending, *exists*.
Not from curiosity, or to practise the heart,
that would also be in the laurel . . .
but because to be here is much, and the transient Here
seems to need and concern us strangely. Us, the most
        transient.
Everyone *once, once* only. Just *once* and no more.
And we also *once*. Never again. But this having been
once, although only *once*, to have been of the earth,
seems irrevocable.

And so we drive ourselves and want to achieve it,
want to hold it in our simple hands,
in the surfeited gaze and in the speechless heart.
Want to become it. Give it to whom? Rather
keep all forever . . . but to the other realm,
alas, what can be taken? Not the power of seeing,
learned here so slowly, and nothing that's happened
        here.
Nothing.

Rainer Maria Rilke

Contents

Prefatory Note

Approaching death, Ernest Becker requested that the original manuscript of this, his final book, rest private and unpublished in a desk drawer, no energy remaining in him for any further barter with the gods. Believing the work to be an eloquent closure of his scientific literary career, Robert Wallace and I (with some initial anguish over the risk of irreverence) firmly decided upon publication realizing that had the time remained, the author himself would have done so for what he considered to be his *magnum opus*. Some material has been eliminated as it appears elsewhere, but beyond editing and routine work the book is Ernest's.

Marie Becker

Preface

This book is a companion volume to *The Denial of Death*. It completes the task begun there, which is to synthesize the scientific and tragic perspectives on man. In *The Denial of Death* I argued that man's innate and all-encompassing fear of death drives him to attempt to transcend death through culturally standardized hero systems and symbols. In this book I attempt to show that man's natural and inevitable urge to deny mortality and achieve a heroic self-image are the root causes of human evil. This book also completes my confrontation of the work of Otto Rank and my attempt to transcribe its relevance for a general science of man. Ideally, of course, the two books should be read side by side in order to give the integrated and comprehensive picture that the author himself has (or imagines he has); but each book stands on its own and can be read without the other.

In my previous writings I tried to sketch out what might be a synthesis of the science of man. One of their major shortcomings, I now see, had to do with their fundamental organizing concept. I thought it was enough to use the unifying "principle of self esteem maintenance." But as we will see in Chapter Five, it was too abstract, it lacked body, a universal, energetic content in the form of specific, inflexible motives. These motives I found in the work of Rank, in his insistence on the fundamental dynamic of the fear of life and death, and man's urge to transcend this fear in a culturally constituted heroism.

My previous writings did not take sufficient account of truly vicious human behavior. This is a dilemma that I have been caught in, along with many others who have been trying to keep alive the Enlightenment tradition of a science of man: how to reflect the empirical data on man, the data that show what a horribly destructive creature he has been throughout his history, and yet still have a science that is not manipulative or cynical. If man is as bad as he seems, then either we have to behaviorally coerce him into the good life or else we have to abandon the hope of a science of man

entirely. This is how the alternatives have appeared. Obviously it
is an enormous problem: to show that man *is* truly evil-causing in
much of his motivation, and yet to move beyond this to the possibilities of sane, renewing action, some kind of third alternative beyond bureaucratic science and despair.

Whether I have succeeded in leaving open the possibility for such
a third alternative, while looking man full in the face for the first
time in my career, is now for others to say. In the process of writing
this book I compiled a pile of slips with things to say in the Preface,
about the matters on which my mind has largely changed, those on
which my views remain the same, etc. But this would be redundant;
it would be easy for any interested student to trace—if he had the
inclination to—the errors and wanderings, the inevitable record of
personal growth and sobering up that characterize a so-called scientific career. Let me just say that if I have changed my views on
many things, this change leaves intact, I believe, the basic premise
of the Enlightenment which I feel we cannot abandon and continue
to be working scientists—namely, that there is nothing in man or
nature which would prevent us from taking some control of our
destiny and making the world a saner place for our children. This
is certainly harder, and more of a gamble, than I once thought; but
maybe this should reinforce our dedication and truly tax our imaginations. Many of us have been lazy or smug, others too hopeful
and naive. The realism of the world should make us better scientists. There is a distinct difference between pessimism, which does
not exclude hope, and cynicism, which does. I see no need, therefore, to apologize for the relative grimness of much of the thought
contained in this book; it seems to me to be starkly empirical.
Since I have been fighting against admitting the dark side of human nature for a dozen years, this thought can hardly be a simple
reflex of my own temperament, of what I naturally feel comfortable
with. Nor is it a simple function of our uneasy epoch, since it was
gathered by the best human minds of many dispositions and epochs,
and so I think it can be said that it reflects objectively the universal
situation of the creature we call man.

Finally, it goes without saying that this is a large project for one
mind to try to put between two covers; I am painfully aware that
I may not have succeeded, that I may have bitten off too much

and may have tried to put it too sparely so that it could all fit in. As in most of my other work, I have reached far beyond my competence and have probably secured for good a reputation for flamboyant gestures. But the times still crowd me and give me no rest, and I see no way to avoid ambitious synthetic attempts; either we get some kind of grip on the accumulation of thought or we continue to wallow helplessly, to starve amidst plenty. So I gamble with science and write, but the game seems to me very serious and necessary.

Research on the book was aided by Simon Fraser University President's Research Grants.

Vancouver, 1972

E.B.

The Human Condition:
Between Appetite and Ingenuity

What could we say in the simplest possible way that would "reveal" man to us—show what he was, what he was trying to do, and what it all added up to? I have been working on this for some years now, trying to make complex things more clear, to peel away disguises and marginalia, trying to get at the truly basic things about man, the things that really drive him. I now see that we must make a clear distinction between man's creatureliness—his appetite—on the one hand and his ingenuity on the other.

Man is an animal. The upshot of the modern body of work called *ethology*, of Lionel Tiger, Robin Fox, Konrad Lorenz, and a host of others, is that it reminds us of the basic human condition: that man is first and and foremost an animal moving about on a planet shining in the sun. Whatever else he is, is built on this. The argument of these people is that we shall never understand man if we do not begin with his animal nature. And this is truly basic. The only *certain* thing we know about this planet is that it is a theater for crawling life, organismic life, and at least we know what organisms are and what they are trying to do.

At its most elemental level the human organism, like crawling life, has a mouth, digestive tract, and anus, a skin to keep it intact, and appendages with which to acquire food. Existence, for all organismic life, is a constant struggle to feed—a struggle to incorporate whatever other organisms they can fit into their mouths and press down their gullets without choking. Seen in these stark terms, life on this planet is a gory spectacle, a science-fiction nightmare in which digestive tracts fitted with teeth at one end are tearing away at whatever flesh they can reach, and at the other end are piling up the fuming waste excrement as they move along in search of more flesh. I think this is why the epoch of the dinosaurs exerts such a

1

strange fascination on us: it is an epic food orgy with king-size actors who convey unmistakably what organisms are dedicated to. Sensitive souls have reacted with shock to the elemental drama of life on this planet, and one of the reasons that Darwin so shocked his time—and still bothers ours—is that he showed this bone-crushing, blood-drinking drama in all its elementality and necessity: Life cannot go on without the mutual devouring of organisms. If at the end of each person's life he were to be presented with the living spectacle of all that he had organismically incorporated in order to stay alive, he might well feel horrified by the living energy he had ingested. The horizon of a gourmet, or even the average person, would be taken up with hundreds of chickens, flocks of lambs and sheep, a small herd of steers, sties full of pigs, and rivers of fish. The din alone would be deafening. To paraphrase Elias Canetti, each organism raises its head over a field of corpses, smiles into the sun, and declares life good.

Beyond the toothsome joy of consuming other organisms is the warm contentment of simply continuing to exist—continuing to experience physical stimuli, to sense one's inner pulsations and mus-culature, to delight in the pleasures that nerves transmit. Once the or-ganism is satiated, this becomes its frantic all-consuming task, to hold onto life at any cost—and the costs can be catastrophic in the case of man. This absolute dedication to Eros, to perseverance, is universal among organisms and is the essence of life on this earth, and be-cause we are mystified by it we call it the instinct for self-preserva-tion. For man, in the words of the anthropologist A. M. Hocart, this organismic craving takes the form of the search for "prosperity"— the universal ambition of human society. Now, prosperity means simply that a high level of organismic functioning will be main-tained, and so anything that works against this has to be avoided. In other words, in man the search for appetitive satisfaction has be-come conscious: he is an organism who *knows* that he wants food and who *knows* what will happen if he doesn't get it, or if he gets it but falls ill and fails to enjoy its benefits. Once we have an animal who recognizes that he needs prosperity, we also have one who realizes that anything that works against continued prosperity is bad. And so we understand how man has come, universally, to identify disease and death as the two principal evils of the human organismic condition. Disease defeats the joys of prosperity while one is alive, and death cuts prosperity off coldly.

Extinction: The Dread of Insignificance

And this brings us to the unique paradox of the human condition: that man wants to persevere as does any animal or primitive organism; he is driven by the same craving to consume, to convert energy, and to enjoy continued experience. But man is cursed with a burden no animal has to bear: he is conscious that his own end is inevitable, that his stomach will die.

Wanting nothing less than eternal prosperity, man from the very beginning could not live with the prospect of death. As I argued in *The Denial of Death,* man erected cultural symbols which do not age or decay to quiet his fear of his ultimate end—and of more immediate concern, to provide the promise of indefinite duration. His culture gives man an alter-organism which is more durable and powerful than the one nature endowed him with. The Muslim heaven, for example, is probably the most straightforward and unselfconscious vision of what the human organism really hopes for, what the alter-organism hopes to enjoy.

What I am saying is that man transcends death via culture not only in simple (or simple-minded) visions like gorging himself with lamb in a perfumed heaven full of dancing girls, but in much more complex and symbolic ways. Man transcends death not only by continuing to feed his appetites, but especially by finding a meaning for his life, some kind of larger scheme into which he fits: he may believe he has fulfilled God's purpose, or done his duty to his ancestors or family, or achieved something which has enriched mankind. This is how man assures the expansive meaning of his life in the face of the real limitations of his body; the "immortal self" can take very spiritual forms, and spirituality is not a simple reflex of hunger and fear. It is an expression of the will to live, the burning desire of the creature to count, to make a difference on the planet because he has lived, has emerged on it, and has worked, suffered, and died.[1]

When Tolstoy came to face death, what he really experienced was anxiety about the meaning of his life. As he lamented in his *Confession:*

What will come of my whole life. . . . Is there any meaning in my life that the inevitable death awaiting me does not destroy?[2]

This is mankind's age-old dilemma in the face of death: it is the meaning of the thing that is of paramount importance; what man really fears is not so much extinction, but extinction *with insignificance.* Man wants to know that his life has somehow counted, if not for himself, then at least in a larger scheme of things, that it has left a trace, a trace that has meaning. And in order for anything once alive to have meaning, its effects must remain alive in eternity in some way. Or, if there is to be a "final" tally of the scurrying of man on earth—a "judgment day"—then this trace of one's life must enter that tally and put on record who one was and that what one did was significant.

We can see that the self-perpetuation of organisms is the basic motive for what is most distinctive about man—namely, religion. As Otto Rank put it, all religion springs, in the last analysis, "not so much from . . . fear of natural death as of final destruction."[3] But it is culture itself that embodies the transcendence of death in some form or other, whether it appears purely religious or not. It is very important for students of man to be clear about this: culture itself is sacred, since *it* is the "religion" that assures in some way the perpetuation of its members. For a long time students of society liked to think in terms of "sacred" versus "profane" aspects of social life. But there has been continued dissatisfaction with this kind of simple dichotomy, and the reason is that there is really no basic distinction between sacred and profane in the symbolic affairs of men. As soon as you have symbols you have artificial self-transcendence via culture. Everything cultural is fabricated and given meaning by the mind, a meaning that was not given by physical nature. Culture is in this sense "supernatural,"[4] and all systematizations of culture have in the end the same goal: to raise men above nature, to assure them that in some ways their lives count in the universe more than merely physical things count.

Now we can get to the point of this brief Introduction and see where it has all been leading. The reader has surely already seen the rub, and objected in his own mind that the symbolic denial of mortality is a figment of the imagination for flesh-and-blood organisms, that if man seeks to avoid evil and assure his eternal prosperity, he is living a fantasy for which there is no scientific evidence so far. To which I would add that this would be all right if the fantasy were a harmless one. The fact is that self-transcendence via culture does not give man a simple and straightforward solution to the problem of death; the terror of death still rumbles underneath the cultural repression (as I argued in a previous book).[5] What men have done is to shift the fear of death onto the higher level of cultural perpetuity; and this very triumph ushers in an ominous new problem. Since men must now hold for dear life onto the self-transcending meanings of the society in which they live, onto the immortality symbols which guarantee them indefinite duration of some kind, a new kind of instability and anxiety are created. And this anxiety is precisely what spills over into the affairs of men. In seeking to avoid evil, man is responsible for bringing more evil into the world than organisms could ever do merely by exercising their digestive tracts. It is man's ingenuity, rather than his animal nature, that has given his fellow creatures such a bitter earthly fate. This is the main argument of my book, and in the following chapters I want to try to show exactly how this comes about, how man's impossible hopes and desires have heaped evil in the world.

CHAPTER ONE

The Primitive World:
Ritual as Practical Technics

*The object of ritual is to secure full life and to
escape from evil. . . .*
A. M. Hocart[1]

One can read anthropology for years—even the very best anthropology—without ever really understanding what men are trying to do in primitive society. There are so many facts, so many strange customs, and they give a picture so complex and overflowing that there doesn't seem to be a center anywhere, and so we can't get any conceptual grip on the phenomenon. Even the voluminous brilliance of a Lévi-Strauss never really tells us *why* primitives are doing such complex and ingenious intellectual work. I have read only one anthropologist who has given us the larger view of the primitive world—A. M. Hocart. It is true that Johan Huizinga came close in his *Homo Ludens*, but Hocart, with his wealth of anthropological data and detail, has brought us to the heart of the matter.

Hocart, as I have said, saw the universal human ambition as the achievement of prosperity—the good life. To satisfy this craving, only man could create that most powerful concept which has both made him heroic and brought him utter tragedy—the invention and practice of ritual, which is first and foremost a technique for promoting the good life and averting evil. Let us not rush over these words: ritual is *a technique for giving life*. The thing is momentous: throughout vast ages of prehistory mankind imagined that it could *control life!* We scoff at the idea because we do not believe life can be controlled by charms, spells, and magic. But as Hocart warns us, just that we do not believe in the efficacy of the technique is no reason for overlooking the momentous place that ritual has had in the life of mankind.[2]

The fact is that primitive man imagined he could transfer life from one thing to another, that he could, for example, take the spirit-power that resided in the scalp of an enemy and, by proper dancing and chanties, transfer that life from its former owner to the new one. Or, in the famous totemic increase ceremonies of the Australian aborigines, primitive men imagined that by going through the motions of imitating animal births they could increase the number of kangaroos, emus, grubs in the world. The technique was so precise that the aborigine could even prescribe the color of the kangaroos—brown, say, rather than gray. Or again, the aim of the technique could be general and vast, and make the renovation of the whole universe, the sun, and all the earth. Or, finally, ritual could generate not only bears or yams, or the life of the whole universe, but the individual soul as well. This is the meaning of the "rites of passage" rituals which took place at birth, puberty, marriage, and death: by means of symbolically dying and being reborn via ritual the individual was elevated to new states of being. Life was not a curve as we see it, where birth is zero and death a return to zero. For primitive man birth was zero, but very often death was considered the final promotion of the soul to a state of superhuman power and indefinite durability.

I'm sure I don't have to expand on any of this—the literature is familiar to most readers, and in any case there is no substitute for reading the details in Hocart, Mircea Eliade, Henri Frankfort, Jane Harrison, or any of a number of such regaling authorities. The point I want to make is very simple and direct: that by means of the techniques of ritual men imagined that they took firm control of the material world, and at the same time transcended that world by fashioning their own invisible projects which made them supernatural, raised them over and above material decay and death. In the world of ritual there aren't even any accidents, and accidents, as we know, are the things that make life most precarious and meaningless. Our knees grow weak when we think of a young girl of awesome beauty who gets crushed to death simply because her foot slips on a mountain path; if life can be so subject to chance, it mustn't have too much meaning. But how can that be, since we are alive and since creatures are so marvelous? Primitive man takes care of this problem by imagining that his control over nature is fairly complete, and that in any case nothing ever happens unless somebody wants it to happen. So a person slips on a mountain path because some powerful dead spirit is jealous of the living, or some witch is secretly working her ritual against that person.[3]

As I see it, the history of mankind divides into two great periods: the first one existed from time immemorial until roughly the Renaissance or Enlightenment, and it was characterized by the ritualist view of nature. The second period began with the efflorescence of the modern machine age and the domination of the scientific method and world view. In both periods men wanted to control life and death, but in the first period they had to rely on a nonmachine technology to do it: ritual is actually a preindustrial *technique of manufacture;* it doesn't exactly create new things, Hocart says, but it transfers the power of life and it renovates nature. But how can we have a technique of manufacture without machinery? Precisely by building a ritual altar and making that the locus of the transfer and renewal of life power:

Unable to take down, repair, and put together again the actual machinery [of the world] when it goes wrong, [the ritualist] . . . takes to pieces and rebuilds their form by means of the [ritual] sacrifice.[4]

If the altar represents a person's body (the machinery) that body may function well or poorly depending how carefully the altar has been constructed. As Hocart adds—and as Lévi-Strauss has recently conclusively argued—there is no need to postulate a mind differently constituted from our own. Man controls nature by whatever he can invent, and primitive man invented the ritual altar and the magical paraphernalia to make it work. And as the modern mechanic carries around his tools, so did the primitive scrupulously transport his charms and rebuild his altars.

We call it magic because we don't believe it worked, and we call our technology scientific because we believe it works. I am not pretending that primitive magic is as efficacious for the control of nature as is our science, but in our time we are beginning to live with some strange and uncomfortable realizations. Primitive ritual manufacture of life may not have actually controlled the universe, but at least it was never in any danger of destroying it. We control it up to a point—the point at which we seem to be destroying it. Besides, our belief in the efficacy of the machine control of nature has in itself elements of magic and ritual trust. Machines are supposed to work, and to work infallibly, since we have to put all our trust in them. And so when they fail to work our whole world view begins to crumble—just as the primitives' world view did when they found their rituals were not working in the face of western culture and weaponry. I am thinking of how anxious we are to find the exact cause of an airplane crash, or how eager we are to attribute the crash to "human error" and not machine failure. Or even more, how the Russians hush up their air crashes: how can machines fail in machine paradise?

The fact that western man didn't know what was going on because he was faced with a technics so alien to his ways of thought probably explains our long puzzlement over the organization of primitive society. The Australian aborigines—who were living in the Stone Age—seemed the most paradoxical of all, with their luxuriant systems of kinship classification and their complex divisions of their tribe into half and half and then half again.

This passion for splitting things into two polar opposites that were complementary was a most striking and widespread feature of primitive man's social organization. (The Chinese Yin and Yang is a survival of this phenomenon.) A person belonged either to one half or the other, traced his descent from a common ancestor, often identified with a particular animal totem representing his half, usually married someone in the other half, and had rigorously specified types of relationship with people in the other half, including the duty to bury them and mourn for them. One of the main things that took place between the halves was something *Homo sapiens* seems to thrive on: contests of skill and excellence. Hocart thinks that the teasing and mocking behaviors which anthropologists call "joking relationships" may have had their origin there. In fact, it is possible that all team games arose out of the dual organization.

Actually the puzzlement mentioned earlier continued until just yesterday. It was laid to rest when Lévi-Strauss tackled head on the luxuriance of primitive symbolism and classification.[5] The result was the complete, widespread, and popular recognition of something anthropologists among themselves had long known: that the primitive mind was just as intelligent as ours, just as intent on examining the minute facts of existence and putting order into them. Primitive man fed into his cerebral computer all the important natural facts of this world as he observed and understood them, and tried to relate them intimately to his life just as we try to relate the mechanical laws of the universe to our own. Did we wonder at the complexity of primitive symbolism and social organization? Well, it was because primitive man tried to organize his society to reflect his theory of nature.

To quote Huizinga:

Anthropology has shown with increasing clarity how social life in the archaic period normally rests on the antagonistic and antithetical structure of the community itself, and how the whole mental world of such a community corresponds to this profound dualism.[6]

Technically we call it "moiety" organization—a dry and forbidding anthropological term that makes the study of primitives so dull, until we give the term life by showing what it means and does. Hocart thought that moiety organization had been nearly universal at some stage of social evolution. Lévi-Strauss too was taken with what he regarded as a natural tendency of the human mind to split things into contrasts and complementarities, which he called "binary opposition." It has given a great boost to the computer freaks, this binary tendency of the primitive mind, because it seems to show that man functions naturally just like the computer—and so the computer can be championed as the logical fulfillment of basic human nature, and the mystery of mind and symbolism might well be traceable down to simple neural circuits, etc.

But Hocart did not get carried away into abstractions as many did. His explanation for this profound dualism lies in the real world of human ambitions and hopes:

Perhaps it is a law of nature, but that is not sufficient to explain the dual organization. . . . Nor does it explain the curious interaction of the moieties; in fact it is this interaction which must explain the dual division; for men divide themselves into two groups in order that they may impart life to one another, that they may intermarry, compete with one another, make offerings to one another, and do to one another whatever is required by their theory of prosperity.[7]

There we have it. Leave it to Hocart to cut through to the heart of the matter. The reason for the dual organization is so foreign to us that we may not at first see it: it was necessary for ritual. The fundamental imperative of all ritual is that one cannot do it alone; man cannot impart life to himself but must get it from his fellow man. If ritual is a technique for generating life, then ritual organization is a necessary cooperation in order to make that technique work.[8]

The deeper level of explanation for the dual organization is so simple we may not see it: it is phenomenological. Man needs to work his magic with the materials of this world, and human beings are the primary materials for the magic wrought by social life. We saw in the Introduction that one of the main motives of organismic life was the urge to self-feeling, to the heightened sense of self that comes with success in overcoming obstacles and incorporating other organisms. The expansion of the self feeling in nature can come about in many different ways, especially when we get to the human level of complexity. Man can expand his self-feeling not only by physical incorporation but by any kind of triumph or demonstration of his own excellence. He expands his organization in complexity by games, puzzles, riddles, mental tricks of all types; by boasting about his achievements, taunting and humiliating his adversaries, or torturing and killing them. Anything that *reduces* the other organisms and adds to one's own size and importance is a direct way to gain self-feeling; it is a natural development out of the simple incorporation and fighting behavior of lower organisms.

By the time we get to man we find that he is in an almost constant struggle not to be *diminished* in his organismic importance. But as he is also and especially a symbolic organism, this struggle against being diminished is carried on on the most minute levels of symbolic complexity. To be outshone by another is to be attacked at some basic level of organismic durability. To lose, to be second rate, to fail to keep up with the best and the highest sends a message to the nerve center of the organism's anxiety: "I am overshadowed, inadequate; hence I do not qualify for continued durability, for life, for eternity; hence I will die." William James saw this everyday anxiety over failure and recorded it with his usual pungent prose:

Failure, then failure! so the world stamps us at every turn. We strew it with our blunders, our misdeeds, our lost opportunities, with all the memorials of our inadequacy to our vocation. And with what a damning emphasis does it then blot us out! . . . The subtlest forms of suffering known to man are connected with the poisonous humiliations incidental to these results. . . . And they are pivotal human experiences. A process so ubiquitous and everlasting is evidently an integral part of life.[9]

We just saw why: because it is connected to the fundamental motive of organismic appetite: to endure, to continue experiencing, and to know that one can continue because he possesses some special excellence that makes him immune to diminution and death.

This explains too the ubiquitousness of envy. Envy is the signal of danger that the organism sends to itself when a shadow is being cast over it, when it is threatened with being diminished. Little wonder that Leslie Farber could call envy a primary emotional substratum, or that Helmut Schoeck could write a whole stimulating book about envy as a central focus of social behavior.[10] The "fear of being reduced . . . almost seems to have a life of its own inside one's being," as Alan Harrington so well put it in a couple of brilliant pages on envy.[11]

I am making this little detour into phenomenological ontology only to remind the reader of the great stake that the organism has in blowing itself up in size, importance, and durability. Because only if we understand how natural this motive is can we understand how it is only in society that man can get the symbolic measures for the *degrees* of his importance, his qualification for extradurability. And it is only by contrasting and comparing himself to *like* organisms, to his fellow men, that he can judge if he has some extra claim to importance. Obviously it is not very convincing about one's ultimate worth to be better than a lobster, or even a fox; but to outshine "that fellow sitting over there, the one with the black eyes"—now that is something that carries the conviction of ultimacy. To paraphrase Buber, the faces of men carry the highest meaning to other men.

Once we understand this, we can see further why the moiety organization is such a stroke 'of primitive genius: it sets up society as a continuing contest for the forcing of self-feeling, provides ready-made props for self-aggrandizement, a daily script that includes straight men for "joking relationships" and talented rivals with whom to contend for social honor in games, feats of strength, hunting and warfare. Sociologists have very nicely described the dynamics of "status forcing" and similar types of behavior, in which people try to come out of social encounters a little bigger than they went in, by playing intricate games of oneupmanship. But you cannot force your status vis-à-vis someone else unless there is a someone else and there are rules for status and verbal conventions for playing around with status, for coming out of social groups with increased self-inflation. Society almost everywhere provides codes for such self-aggrandizement, for the ability to boast, to humiliate, or just simply to outshine in quiet ways—like displaying one's superior achievements, even if it is only skill in hunting that feeds everyone's stomach. If Hocart says that man cannot impart life to himself but must get it via ritual from his fellow man, then we can say even further that man cannot impart importance to himself; and importance, we now see, is just as deep a problem in securing life: importance equals durability equals life.

However, I don't want to seem to be making out that primitive society organized itself merely as a stage for competitive self-aggrandizement, or that men can only expand their sense of self at the expense of others. This would not be true, even though it is a large and evidently natural part of human motivation. Primitive society also expressed its genius by giving to people much less invidious and competitive forms of self-expansion. I think here of the work of Erving Goffman, in which he showed with such consummate art how people impart to one another the daily sense of importance that each needs, not with rivalry and boasting, but rather with elaborate rules for protecting their insides against social damage and deflation. People do this in their interpersonal encounters by using verbal formulas that express proper courtesies, permit gentle handling, save the other's "face" with the proper subtleties when self-esteem is in danger, and so on. Social life is interwoven with salutations for greeting and taking leave, for acknowledging others with short, standardized conversations which reinforce the sense of well-being of all the members.[12] There is no point in repeating Goffman here, or even in trying to sum up his approach; all I want to do is to say that men in society manage to give to each other what they need in terms of good organismic self-feeling in two major ways: on one hand, by codes that allow people to compare their achievements and virtues so as to outshine rivals; on the other hand, by codes that support and protect tender human feelings that prevent the undermining and deflation that can result from the clash of organismic ambitions.

But now to see how the technique for the ritual renewal of nature worked—how well it served the actors who played the parts. We can really only get "inside" primitive societies by seeing them as religious priesthoods with each person having a role to play in the generative rituals. We have so long been stripped of a ritual role to play in creation that we have to force ourselves to try to understand this, to get this into perspective. We don't know what it means to contribute a dance, a chant, or a spell in a community dramatization of the forces of nature—unless we belong to an active religious community.* Nor can we feel the immense sense of achievement that follows from such a ritual contribution: the ritualist has done nothing less than enable life to continue; he has contributed to sustaining and renewing the universe. If rituals generate and redistribute life power, then each person is a generator of life. That is how important a person could feel, within the ritualist view of nature, by occupying a ritual place in a community. Even the humblest person was a cosmic creator. We may not think

---

* I think a good case could be made for rock music festivals as the modern popular religious experience, the ultimate degenerate form of the ancient ritual dramatization. Rock serves the same function without the cosmic connection, much as the circus does. See Sidney Tarachow's fine little overview, "Circuses and Clowns," in Géza Róheim, ed., Psychoanalysis and the Social Sciences (New York: International Universities Press, 1951), vol. 3, pp. 171–185, and compare this description with a performance by the Alice Cooper rock group.

that the ritual generation of brown kangaroos is a valid causal affair, but the primitive feels the effect of his ability to generate life, he is ennobled by it, even though it may be an illusion. We may console ourselves about our historical demotion from the status of cosmic heroism by saying that at least we know what true religion is, whereas these cosmic creators lived according to childish magic. I'll admit that our historical disenchantment is a burden that gives us a certain sober worldliness, but there is no valid difference between religion and magic, no matter how many books are written to support the distinction. As Hocart pointed out so succinctly, magic is religion we don't believe in, and religion is magic we believe in. *Voilà tout.*

What Huizinga did in *Homo Ludens* was to show that primitive life was basically a rich and playful dramatization of life; primitive man acted out his significance as a living creature and as a lord over other creatures. It seems to me like genius, this remarkable intuition of what man needs and wants; and primitive man not only had this uncanny intuition but actually acted on it, set up his social life to give himself what he needed and wanted. We may know what we lack in modern life, and we brood on it, but twist and sweat as we may we can never seem to bring it off. Perhaps things were simpler and more manageable in prehistoric times and had not gotten out of hand, and so man could act on what he knew. Primitive man set up his society as a stage, surrounded himself with actors to play different roles, invented gods to address the performance to, and then ran off one ritual drama after the other, raising himself to the stars and bringing the stars down into the affairs of men. He staged the dance of life, with himself at the center. And to think that when western man first crashed uninvited into these spectacular dramas, he was scornful of what he saw. That was because, as Huizinga so well argued, western man was already a fallen creature who had forgotten how to play, how to impart to life high style and significance. Western man was being given a brief glimpse of the creations of human genius, and like a petulant imbecile bully who feels discomfort at what he doesn't understand, he proceeded to smash everything in sight.

Many people have scoffed at Goffman's delineation of the everyday modern rituals of face-work and status forcing; they have argued that these types of petty self-promotion might be true of modern organization men hopelessly set adrift in bureaucratic society but these kinds of shallow oneupmanship behaviors couldn't possibly be true of man everywhere. Consequently, these critics say, Goffman may be a perceptive observer of the contemporary scene, of the one-dimensionality of mass society, but he is definitely not talking about human nature. I have noted elsewhere that I think these critics of Goffman are very wrong, and I repeat it here because it is more in context with the deeper understanding of primitive society. When you set up society to do creation rituals, then you obviously increase geometrically the magnitude of importance that organisms can impart to one another. It is only in modern society that the mutual imparting of self-importance has trickled down to the simple maneuvering of face-work; there is hardly any way to get a sense of value except from the boss, the company dinner, or the random social encounters in the elevator or on the way to the executive toilet. It is pretty demeaning—but that is not Goffman's fault, it is the playing out of the historical decadence of ritual. Primitive society was a formal organization for the apotheosis of man. Our own everyday rituals seem shallow precisely because they lack the cosmic connection. Instead of only using one's fellow man as a mirror to make one's face shine, the primitive used the whole cosmos. I think it is safe to say that primitive organization for ritual is the paradigm and ancestor of all face-work, and that archaic ritual was nothing other than in-depth face-work; it related the person to the mysterious forces of the cosmos, gave him an intimate share in them. This is why the primitive seems multidimensional to many present-day anthropologists who are critical of modern mass society.

So far I have been talking vaguely and in generalities about the "cosmic connection"; I merely mentioned and skipped by the fact that primitive society was organized according to a particular theory of nature, hence the luxuriance of its symbolisms and the formalism of its organization. Now we have to see what this means.

As ritual is an organization for life, it has to be carried out according to a particular theory of prosperity—that is, how exactly to get nature to give more life to the tribe. The most striking thing to us about the primitive theory of prosperity is how elemental it was—or organic, as we would say today. Primitive man observed nature and tried to discern in it what made the dance of life—where the power came from, how things became fecund. If you are going to generate life, you have to determine its principles and imitate the things that embody them. Organisms respond naturally to the sun, which gives heat and light, and find their richness in the earth, which produces food out of nothing—or rather out of its mysterious bowels. The Australian aborigines have an expression about the sun's rays having intercourse with the earth. Very early man seems to have isolated the principles of fecundity and fertilization and tried to promote them by impersonating them. And so men identified with the sky or the heavens, and the earth, and divided themselves into heavenly people and earthly ones. Hocart sums it up nicely:

In cosmic rites the whole world is involved, but in two parts, sky and earth, because all prosperity is conceived to be due to the orderly interaction of sky and earth. The sky alone cannot create, nor the earth alone bring forth. Therefore in the ritual that regulates the world there must be two principles and they must be male and female, for the interplay of the earth and sky is analogous to the intercourse of sexes.[13]

The moieties stood for these opposing yet complementary principles. The world was divided not only into sky and earth but also into right and left, light and darkness, power and weakness—and even life and death.[14] The point was that reality in the round had to be represented in order for it to be controlled. The primitive knew that death was an important part of creation, and so he embodied death in order to control it.

Modern man has long since abandoned the ritual renewal theory of nature, and reality for us is simply refusing to acknowledge that evil and death are constantly with us. With medical science we want to banish death, and so we deny it a place in our consciousness. We are shocked by the vulgarity of symbols of death and the devil and sexual intercourse in primitive ruins. But if your theory is to control by representation and imitation, then you have to include all sides of life, not only the side that makes you comfortable or that seems purest.

There are two words which sum up very nicely what the primitive was up to with his social representation of nature: "microcosmization" and "macrocosmization." Although they sound technically forbidding, they express quite simple complementary maneuvers. In macrocosmization man simply takes himself or parts of himself and blows them up to cosmic importance. Thus the popular ancient pastime of entrail reading or liver reading: it was thought that the fate of the individual, or a whole army or a country, could be discerned in the liver, which was conceived as a small-scale cosmos. The ancient Hindus, among others, looked at every part of man as having a correspondence in the macrocosm: the head corresponded to the sky, the eye to the sun, the breath to the wind, the legs to the earth, and so on.[15] With the universe reflected in his very body, the Hindu thus thought his life had the order of the cosmos.

Microcosmization of the heavens is merely a reverse, complementary movement. Man humanizes the cosmos by projecting all imaginable earthly things onto the heavens, in this way again intertwining his own destiny with the immortal stars. So, for example, animals were projected onto the sky, star formations were given animal shapes, and the zodiac was conceived. By man's transferring animals to heaven all human concerns took on a timelessness and a superhuman validity.

The immortal stars came to preside over human destiny, and the fragile and ephemeral animal called man blew himself up to superhuman size by making himself the center of things. Campsites and buildings were all laid out according to some kind of astronomical plan which intertwined human space with the immortal spheres. The place where the tribe lived was conceived as the navel of the universe where all creative powers poured forth.

For those who want to investigate further the splendid literature on this topic, Rank brilliantly summed up in the 1930s the accumulation of the intensive research of the early decades of the century.[16] All I want to do is to emphasize that by means of micro- and macrocosmization man humanized the heavens and spiritualized the earth and so melted sky and earth together in an inextricable unity. By opposing culture to nature in these ways, man allotted to himself a special spiritual destiny, one that enabled him to transcend his animal condition and assume a special status in nature. No longer was he an animal who died and vanished from the earth; he was a creator of life who could also give eternal life to himself by means of communal rituals of cosmic regeneration.*

And so we have come full circle in our overview of the primitive world. We started with the statement that primitive man used the dual organization to affirm his organismic self-feeling, and one of his principal means was the setting up of society in the form of organized rivalry. Now we can conclude that he in fact set up the whole cosmos in a way that allowed him to expand symbolically and to enjoy the highest organismic pleasures: he could blow the self-feeling of a mere organismic creature all the way up to the stars. The Egyptians hoped that when they died they would ascend to heaven and become stars and thus enjoy eternal significance in the scheme of things. This is already a comedown from what primitive social groupings enjoyed: the daily living of divine significance, the constant meddling into the realm of cosmic power. I said that primitive society was organized for contests and games, as Huizinga showed, but these were not games as we now think of them. They were games as children play them: they actually aimed to control nature, to make things come out as they wanted them. Ritual contests between moieties were a play of life against death, forces of light against forces of darkness. One side tried to thwart the ritual activities of the other and defeat it. But of course the side of life always contrived to win because by this victory primitive man kept nature going in the grooves he needed and wanted. If death and disease were overtaking a people, then

---

* In anthropology Lévi-Strauss has recently revived this opposition of culture to nature, but he is somehow content to leave it as an intellectual problem. Whereas it is obvious—as it was to Rank and Van der Leeuw—that man has something great at stake in this opposition: the control and allaying of creature anxiety. Octavio Paz has understood how central the problem of overcoming death was to the primitive, and has criticized Lévi-Strauss for completely glossing over the vital human motives for primitive man's talent at symbolism. See O. Paz, *Claude Lévi-Strauss* (Ithaca, N.Y.: Cornell University Press, 1970) and also the important attempt to reorient Lévi-Strauss in the direction of the problem of death: J. Fabian, "How Others Die," in Arien Mack, ed., *Social Research* (a publication of the New School for Social Research), 1972, 39, number 3: 543–567.

a ritually enacted reversal of death by a triumph of the life faction would, hopefully, set things right again.[17] *

The Logic of Sacrifice

At the center of the primitive technics of nature stands the act of sacrifice, which reveals the essence of the whole science of ritual; in a way we might see it as the atomic physics of the primitive world view. The sacrificer goes through the motions of performing in miniature the kind of arrangement of nature that he wants. He may use water, clay, and fire to represent the sea, earth, and sun, and he proceeds to set up the creation of the world. If he does things exactly as prescribed, as the gods did them in the beginning of time, then he gets control over the earth and creation. He can put vigor into animals, milk into females, and even arrange the order of society into castes, as in the Hindu ritual.

In the Hindu ritual and in coronation rituals, this is the point at which the contest came in. In order to control nature, man must drive away evil—sickness and death. And so he must overcome demons and hostile forces. If he makes a slip in the ritual, it gives power to the demons. The ritual triumph is thus the winning of a contest with evil. When kings were to be crowned they had to prove their merit by winning out against the forces of evil; dice and chess probably had their origin as the way of deciding whether the king really could outwit and defeat the forces of darkness.[18]

We said earlier that western man did not understand this kind of technics and so he ridiculed it. Hocart comes back again and again to this point, that our notions of what is possible are not the same as those of archaic men. They believed that they could put vigor into the world by means of a ceremony, that they could create

---

* We will see later, when we consider the historical evolution of evil, how fateful these ritual enactments were for the future of mankind. By opposing the forces of light and darkness, and by needing to make light triumph over dark, primitive man was obliged to give the ascendancy to the actors representing light and life. In this way, as we shall see, a natural inequality was built into social organization, and as Hocart so superbly speculates, this gave rise to the evolution of privileged "pure" groups and outcast "evil" ones.

an island, an abundance of creatures, keep the sun on its course, etc.[19] The whole thing seemed ridiculous to us because we looked only at the surface of it and did not see the logic behind it, the *forces* that were really at work according to the primitive's understanding of them. There is no point in my simply repeating Hocart's penetrating analysis of the logic of the equivalence of the sacrificer and the universe.[20] The key idea underlying the whole thing is that as the sacrificer manipulates the altar and the victim, he becomes identified with them—not with them as *things*, but with the essences behind them, their invisible connection to the world of the gods and spirits, to the very insides of nature. And this too is logical. The primitive had a conceptualization of the insides of nature just as we do in our atomic theory. He saw that things were animated by invisible forces, that the sun's heat worked at a distance and pervaded the things of the earth, that seeds germinated out of the invisible as did children, etc. All he wanted to do, with the technique of sacrifice, was to take possession of these invisible forces and use them for the benefit of the community.[21] He had no need for missile launchers and atomic reactors; sacrificial altar mounds served his purposes well.

In a word, the act of sacrifice established a footing in the invisible dimension of reality; this permitted the sacrificer to build a divine body, a mystical, essential self that had superhuman powers. Hocart warns us that if we think this is so foreign to our own traditional ways of thinking, we should look closely at the Christian communion. By performing the prescribed rites the communicant unites himself with Christ—the sacrifice—who is God, and in this way the worshiper accrues to himself a mystical body or soul which has immortal life. Everything depends on the prescribed ritual, which puts one in possession of the power of eternity by union with the sacrifice.

Conclusion

What I have done in these few pages is to try to show that primitive society was organized for a certain kind of production of life, a ritual technique of manufacture of the things of the world that used the dimension of the invisible. Man used his ingenuity to fill his stomach, to get control of nature for the benefit of his organism; this is only logical and natural. But this stomach-centered characteristic of all culture is something we easily lose sight of. One reason is that man was never content to just stop at food: he wanted more life in the widest sense of the term—exactly what we would expect an organism to want if it could somehow contrive to be self-conscious about life and death and the need to continue experiencing.[22] Food is only one part of that quest; man quickly saw beyond mere physical nourishment and had to conceive ways to qualify for immortality. In this way the simple food quest was transmuted into a quest for spiritual excellence, for goodness and purity. All of man's higher spiritual ideals were a continuation of the original quest for energy-power. Nietzsche was one of the first to state this blatantly, and he shocked the world with it: that all morality is fundamentally a matter of power, of the power of organisms to continue existing by reaching for a superhuman purity. It is all right for man to talk about spiritual aims; what he really means is aims for merits that qualify him for eternity. This too, of course, is the logical development of organismic ambitions.

Hocart ends his noted work *Kingship* with just such a commentary on the evolution of spirituality out of the simple quest for physical life:

Thus the sacrificial lamb is no longer the young of an ewe slaughtered at the Paschal Feast as the embodiment of some god in order to promote the life of the crops, but a symbol expressing . . . a sum of innocence, purity, gentleness, self-sacrifice, redemption and divinity. . . . Doubtless many will be scandalized at any attempt to derive the cure of souls from the cravings of the stomach. . . . Even so the rising generation may find cause not for anger, but for wonder, in the rapidity with which Man, so late emerged from the brute, has proceeded from the conquest of matter to that of the spirit.[23]

No one would dare gainsay the profoundly unselfish and spiritual emotions that man is capable of. As a creature he is most attuned to the living miracle of the cosmos and responds to that miracle with a fineness and a nobility that are in themselves wondrous; the whole thing is surely part of a divine mystery. But the step from the stomach quest to the spiritual one is not in itself as idealistic as Hocart would seem to make out. The earning of spiritual points is the initial impetus of the search for purity, however much some few noble souls might transmute that in an unselfish direction. For most men faith in spirituality is merely a step into continued life, the exact extension of the organismic stomach project.

There is a small debate being aired in certain circles of anthropology today about the many ways in which primitive life was superior to our own. Lévi-Strauss himself has taken a stand in favor of the primitive.[24] I don't want to go into the pros and cons of it and the many subtle and valid arguments produced on both sides. But it does help us to understand the primitive world if we agree to the old anthropological tenet about "the psychic unity of mankind"—that is, that man everywhere, no matter how exotic a particular culture, is basically standard vintage *Homo sapiens*, interchangeable in his nature and motives with any other human being. This is what the whole movement to rehabilitate the primitive—from Hocart to Lévi-Strauss—has been about: to show that he is basically no different from ourselves and certainly not inferior mentally or emotionally. Well, having agreed that the primitive is no worse than we are, it might be in order to add that he is no better. Otherwise, as we shall see, we cannot really understand what happened in history, unless we try to make out that a different animal developed, nor can we understand the problems of modern society, unless we pretend that modern man is a wholly degenerate type of *Homo sapiens*.

What I am saying is that if modern man seems mad in his obsession to control nature by technology, primitive man was no less obsessed by his own mystical technics of sacrifice. After all, one of the things we have learned from the modern study of mental illness is that to make the body the referent of the whole cosmos is a technique of madness.[25] It is true that by institutionalizing macrocosmization, primitive man made it a normal way of referring oneself to transcendent events. But this kind of "normality" is itself unreal, it blows man up to an abnormal size, and so we are right to consider it self-defeating, a departure from the truth of the human condition. If the primitive was not less intelligent, he was equally not less intent on self-perpetuation. When we "step off" into history, we seem to see a type of man who is more driven—but this is only because he started off already obsessed with control and with a hunger for immortality. It is true that primitive man was kinder to nature, that he did not cause the kind of destructiveness we are causing and, in fact, did not seem capable of our kind of casual disregard for the bounty of the natural world. It would take a lot of study and compilation of comparative data to bear these impressions out, but I think that if primitive man was kinder to nature, it was not because he was innately different in his emotional sensitivity nor more altruistic toward other living forms than we are. I think, rather, that it was because his technics of manipulation was less destructive. He needed *a* tree, the spirit of *an* animal or plant, the sacrifice of *one* animal of a species. As we shall see, we grind up astronomically larger quantities of life, but it is in the same spirit and for the same basic reasons. If we talk about a certain primitive quality of "reverence" for life, we must be very careful. The primitives' attitude toward animals considered sacred was sometimes more cruel than our own is. They did not hesitate to sacrifice those whom they considered their benefactors or their gods, or even hesitate to kill their chiefs and kings. The main value was whether this brought life to the community and whether the ritual demanded it.[26] Man has always casually sacrificed life for more life.

Probably more to the point, man has always treated with consideration and respect those parts of the natural world over which he has had no control. As soon as he was sure of his powers, his respect for the mystery of what he faced diminished. Hocart makes a telling point about the evolution of man's attitude toward animals:

As his superiority and mastery over the rest of the living world became more and more apparent he seems to have become more and more anxious to disclaim relationship with animals, especially when worship became associated with respect. There is no objection to an animal's being the object of a cult when this does not imply respect but is merely a procedure for causing the animal to multiply. It is a very different thing when ritual becomes worship; man is loath to abase himself before an animal.[27]

Hocart attributes this to "the growing conceit of man." But we could just as well see it as a result of natural narcissism. Each organism preens itself on the specialness of the life that throbs within it, and is ready to subordinate all others to its own continuation. Man was always conceited; he only began to show his destructive side to the rest of nature when the ritual technology of the spiritual production of animals was superseded by other technologies. The unfolding of history is precisely the saga of the succession of new and different ideologies of organismic self-perpetuation—and the new injustices and heightened destructiveness of historical man. Let us turn to this.

CHAPTER TWO

The Primitive World:
Economics as Expiation and Power

Now that we have talked about how primitive man created or
helped create natural bounty, we have to look at what he did with
this bounty, how he applied his concept of the natural order of
things in daily life in addition to performing it in ritual. When we
put these two aspects together, they give us a fairly complete
picture of primitive society, of how man lived through long periods
of prehistory.

It often happens that we get our most important insights from
people outside a field, and anthropology is no exception. Huizinga,
as mentioned, is one such outsider who has helped us understand
primitive society. Norman O. Brown is another; his analysis of
primitive economics literally brims with insights.[1] What makes his
discussion so seminal is that he has combined essential, often
overlooked work from classical anthropology and psychoanalysis in
his analysis of economic motives. But his psychoanalysis, unlike
Róheim's, is not the dogmatic Freudian kind, and it has not been
brought to bear on primitive society in order to prove Freud right.[2]
The whole burden of Brown's argument is to show that economic
activity itself, from the dawn of human society to the present time,
is sacred to the core.[3] It is not a rational, secular activity designed
simply to meet human survival needs. Or, better, it is not *only*
that, never was, and never will be. If it were, how explain man's
drive to create a surplus, from the very beginning of society to the
present? How explain man's willingness to forgo pleasure, to deny
himself, in order to produce beyond his capacity to consume?
Why do people work so hard to create useless goods when they
already have enough to eat? We know that primitives amassed
huge piles of food and other goods often only to ceremoniously
destroy them, just as we continue to do. We know that many of

26

their choicest trade items, such as bits of amber, were entirely superfluous; that many of their most valuable economic possessions created with painstaking labors were practically useless, e.g., the big ceremonial axe-blade of the Trobriands. And finally we know that historically this creation of useless goods got out of hand and led to the present plight of men—immersed in a horizon of polluting junk, besieged by social injustice and class and race oppression, haves and have-nots, all grasping, fighting, shoving, not knowing how they got into their abysmal condition or what it all means. Let us now turn to what is probably one of the most vital chapters in man's self-understanding.

Economics as Expiation

What was the "economic" activity most characteristic of primitive society? Marcel Mauss revealed it a half century ago in his famous study *The Gift*.[4] There he showed, from a sample of many diverse societies, that the giving of gifts between groups and individuals was the heart of archaic social systems. On the primitive level we see compellingly that social life is a continual dialogue of gift giving and counter gift giving.

To the anthropological observer the thing was simply marvelous: goods were shared and freely given; men observed the principle of social reciprocity and respected social obligations to the letter. When there was food, there was food for all; the hunter who killed the game distributed it with pride and often took the least desirable part of the animal for himself. As Brown says, this was the core of truth in the myth of primitive communism. If someone had something you wanted, you asked for it and received it. But often this continuous gift giving and taking seemed to the western observer to be perverse; a native would work very hard at the trading post to earn a shirt, and when he came back a week later someone else would be wearing it. Westerners could only think that this represented a basic lack of responsibility, a kind of simple-mindedness. It is so alien to our "I got mine—you get yours" philosophy. Or more alarmingly, missionaries would find that natives came to their hut and simply took valuable knives, guns, clothes, etc., without so much as a "thank you," as though these were coming to them.

How could traders, missionaries, and administrators understand something that often eluded anthropologists themselves: that primitive man did not act out of economic principles, that the process of freely giving and receiving was embedded in a much larger, much more important cosmology, that since the white man had destroyed the old gods and replaced them, he had to give freely just as the gods had done. Primitive life was openly immersed in debt, in obligation to the invisible powers, the ancestors, the dead souls; the group lived partly by drawing its powers from the non-living. Unlike us, primitives knew the truth of man's relation to nature: nature gives freely of its bounty to man—this was the miracle for which to be grateful and beholden and give to the gods of nature in return. Whatever one received was already a gift, and so to keep things in balance one had to give in return—to one another and, by offerings, to the spirits. The gods existed in order to receive gifts. This helps us understand why primitive society seems so "masochistic" to us in its willing submission to nature and to dead spirits. It had found the perfect formula for keeping things in balance:

In the archaic consciousness the sense of indebtedness exists together with the illusion that the debt is payable; the gods exist to make the debt payable. Hence the archaic economy is embedded in religion, limited by the religious framework, and mitigated by the consolations of religion—above all, removal of indebtedness and guilt.[5]

And this explains too the thing that has puzzled thinkers since the beginning of the study of man: why weren't natives content to live in the primitive "paradise," why couldn't man simply relax and consume nature's bounty, why was he driven from the very beginning to develop a surplus beyond basic human needs? The answer is that primitive man created an economic surplus so that he would have *something to give* to the gods; the giving of the surplus was an offering to the gods who controlled the entire economy of nature in the first place, and so man *needed* to give precisely in order to keep himself immersed in the cosmology of obligation and expiation. The ceremonial destruction of mountains of precious food was just that: a ceremonial, religious act. The painstaking fabrication of charms or the dangerous hunting down of rare objects like whale's teeth represented the sweat of one's brow for the most vital motive man knew: to keep the cycle of power moving from the invisible to the visible world. When man gives, "the stream of life continues to flow," as Van der Leeuw so beautifully summed it up in his classic study of primitive ideas.[6] In order to understand this, we have to abandon our own notions of what a gift is. It is not a bribe by one who is a stranger to you and simply wants to "get in good" with you, or by a loved one who wants to draw close to you or even selflessly give you pleasure.

Economics as Power

In the first place, for the primitive the gift was a part of the stream of nature's bounty. Many people today think that the primitive saw the world more under the aspect of miracle and awe than we do, and so he appreciated elemental things more than we do. In order to recapture this way of looking at nature, we moderns usually have to experience a breakdown and rebirth into naive perception. So, for example, when Hamann was asked what Christianity meant to him, he said it was a search for the elements of bread and wine. But we don't need to romanticize about the primitive (whether truly or not) in order to understand his valuation of nature's bounty. We saw that the main organismic motive was self-perpetuation; it is logical that when self-perpetuation became a conscious problem at the level of man he naturally tended to value those things that gave him the power to endure, those things that incorporated the sun's energy and that gave warmth and life. Food is a sacred element because it gives the power of life. The original sacrifice is always food because this is what one wants from the gods as the basis for life. "Give us our daily bread. . . ." Furthermore, if food contains power, it is always more than itself, more than a physical thing: it has a mysterious inner essence or spirit. Milk is the essence of the cow, shark's teeth are the essence of the shark's vitality and murderousness, etc. So when primitive man gave these things as gifts, he did not give a dead thing, a mere object as it appears to us—but a piece of life, of spirit, even a part of himself because he was immersed in the stream of life. The gifts had mana power, the strength of supernatural life.

This is what made the bond and allowed the stream to flow between giver and receiver: to give and then to counter-give kept the motion going, preserved the cycle of power. This is how we are to understand the potlatch giving and oneupmanship, the destruction of quantities of goods: the eternal flux of power in the broad stream of life was generated by the *greatest possible expenditure;* man wanted that stream to flow as bountifully as possible.[7] It then became hard to distinguish who gave and who received, since all were bathed in the power of the movement: everyone participated in the powers that were opened up—the giver, the community, the gods. "I give you power so that you may have power." The more you give, the more everyone gets.

This feeling of expenditure as power is not strange to us moderns either. We want to keep our goods moving with the same obsessive dedication—cars, refrigerators, homes, money. We feel that there is health and strength in the world if the economy *moves,* if there is a frenzy of buying and trading on the stock market, activity in the banks; and this is not only because the movement of goods piles up money in the bank, but actually reflects, I think, the sense of trust and security that the magical free-enterprise powers are working for us so long as we continue to buy, sell, and move goods. The Soviets are experiencing the same thing: the sense of exhilaration and self-celebration in the movement of production and consumption of goods. Like the primitive, modern man feels that he can prosper only *if he shows that he already has* power. Yet of course in its one-dimensionality this is a caricature on the primitive potlatch, as most of modern power ideology is; it has no anchor in the invisible world, in the deference to the gods. Primitive man gave *to* the gods. Hocart sees this as the origin of trade: the fact that one group made offerings to the gods of their kinsmen and vice versa. This led to the exchange of different stuffs between different groups, and in it we see the direct motive of the creation of a surplus for exchange. The exchange of offerings was always a kind of contest—who could give the most to the gods of their kinsmen. We can see what this did for a person: it gave him a contest in which he could be victorious if his offerings of surplus exceeded those of the other clan. In a word, it gave him cosmic heroism, the distinction of releasing the most power in nature for the benefit of all. He was a hero in the eyes not only of the gods but also of men; he earned social honor, "the right to crow."[8] He was a "big power" man. Thus we can see in gift giving and potlatch the continuation of the triumph of the hunter, but now in the creation and distribution of one's own fabricated surplus. Róheim very aptly called this state of things "narcissistic capitalism": the equation of wealth with magic power.[9] And so all this seemingly useless surplus, dangerously and painstakingly wrought, yields the highest usage of all in terms of *power*. Man, the animal who knows he is not safe here, who needs continued affirmation of his powers, is the one animal who is implacably driven to work beyond animal needs precisely because he is not a secure animal. The origin of human drivenness is *religious* because man experiences creatureliness; the amassing of a surplus, then, goes to the very heart of human motivation, the urge to stand out as a hero, to transcend the limitations of the human condition and achieve victory over impotence and finitude.

We see, too, as Brown says, that in the strict utilitarian sense in which we understand the term, primitive "work" cannot be economic; for instance, our "common ownership" and "collective enterprise" in which the person is a "partner" do not do justice to the multidimensionality of the primitive world. Primitive man worked so that he could win a contest in which the offering was made to the gods; he got spiritual merit for his labors. I suppose early Calvinism was an echo of this performance for the eyes of men and the gods, but without the continual giving, the redistribution of the most precious goods. "Big men" in primitive society were those who gave away the most, had nothing for themselves. Sometimes a chief would even offer his own life to appease an injured party in a quarrel; his role was often nothing else than to be a vehicle for the smooth flow of life in the tribe. (The resemblance to historical Calvinism ends abruptly at this kind of performance for spiritual merit.) This reveals a central fact about social life: *primitive man* immersed *himself* in a network of social obligations for psychological reasons. Just as Rank said, man has to have a core psychological motive for being in the group in the first place, otherwise he would not be a group-living animal. Or as Brown, who likes to call a spade a spade, put it, "man entered social organization in order to share guilt. Social organization . . . is a structure of shared guilt . . . a symbolic mutual confession of guilt."[10] And so in one sweep we can understand how primitive economics is inexorably sacred, communal, and yet psychologically motivated at the same time.

The Nature of Guilt

But this kind of picture risks putting primitive man even further beyond our comprehension, even though it seems logically to explain what he was doing. The problem is in the key motive, guilt. Unless we have a correct feeling for what guilt is, what the experience of it means, the sacred nature of primitive economics may escape us. We may even prefer our illusionless "economic man" to the "pitiful" primitives—and this result will entirely undo Brown's thesis. But he himself is in some measure to blame. He draws partly on Nietzsche and Freud, and some of their scorn of guilt as a weakness seems to have rubbed off on him. Even more seriously, by his own admission he does not have any theory of the nature of guilt ("Whatever the ultimate explanation of guilt may be . . .")[11] even though he bases his whole argument on it. When he does offer one explanation, he makes of guilt a simple reflex of the repression of enjoyment—something for which he has already so well castigated Freud in discussing the problem of anality: "The repression of full enjoyment in the present inevitably releases aggression against those ancestors out of love of whom the repression was instituted. Aggression against those simultaneously loved is guilt."[12]

This is *one* explanation of guilt that comes from psychoanalysis:

the child in his boundless desires for gratification can't help feeling love for those who respond to him; at the same time, when they inevitably frustrate him for his own good, he can't help feeling hate and destructive impulses toward them, which puts him in an impossible bind. The bind is one kind of guilt, but only one aspect of the *total bind of life* which constitutes the immense burden of guilt on the human psyche.*

One of the reasons guilt is so difficult to analyze is that it is itself "dumb." It is a feeling of being blocked, limited, transcended, without knowing why. It is the peculiar experience of an organism which can apprehend a totality of things and not be able to move in relation to it. Man experiences this uniquely as a feeling of the crushing awesomeness of things and his helplessness in the face of them. This real guilt partly explains man's willing subordinacy to his culture; after all, the world of men is even more dazzling and miraculous in its richness than the awesomeness of nature. Also, subordinacy comes naturally from man's basic experiences of being nourished and cared for; it is a logical response to social altruism. Especially when one is sick or injured, he experiences the healing forces as coming from the superordinate cultural system of tools, medicines, and the hard-won skills of persons. An attitude of humble gratitude is a logical one to assume toward the forces that sustain one's life; we see this very plainly in the learning and development of children.

Another reason that guilt is so diffuse is that it is many different things: there are many different binds in life. One can be in a bind in relation to one's own development, can feel that one has not achieved all one should have. One can be in a bind in relation to one's body, which is the guilt of anality: to feel bound and doomed by one's physical appendages and orifices. Man also experiences guilt because he takes up space and has unintended effects on others—for example, when we hurt others without intending to, just by being what we are or by following our natural desires and appetites, not to mention when we hurt others physically by accident or thoughtlessness. This, of course, is part of the guilt of our bodies, which have effects that we do not intend in

---

* Here I am obliged to repeat things I have written elsewhere on guilt partly because they are essential to understanding the primitive and partly because, like Brown, I am having a dialogue with myself.

our inner selves. To use Rank's happy phrase, this is guilt we feel for being a "fate-creating" object.[13] We feel guilt in relation to what weighs on us, a weight that we sense is more than we can handle, and so our wives and children are a burden of guilt because we cannot possibly foresee and handle all the accidents, sicknesses, etc., that can happen to them; we feel limited and bowed down, we can't be as carefree and self-expansive as we would like, the world is too much with us.[14]

If we feel guilt when we have not developed our potential, we also are put into a bind by developing too much. Our own uniqueness becomes a burden to us; we "stick out" more than we can safely manage. Guilt makes sense in relation to evolution itself. Man is on the "cutting edge" of evolution; he is the animal whose development is not prefigured by instincts, and so he is open to becoming what he can. This means literally that each person is already somewhat "ahead of himself" simply by virtue of being human and not animal. No wonder people have almost universally feared the "evil eye" in traditional society: it expresses a natural and age-old reaction to making oneself too prominent, detaching oneself too much from the background of things. In traditional Jewish culture, for example, each time the speaker made a favorable remark about the health or achievement of someone dear to him, he immediately followed this remark with the invocation *"Kein Ayin-Hara"* (no evil eye), as if to say "may this good fortune and prominence not be undone by being too conspicuous." Some individuals achieve an intensity of individuation in which they stick out so far that almost each day is an unbearable exposure. But even the average person in any society is already more of an individual than any animal can be; the testimonial to this is in the human face, which is the most individuated animal expression in nature. Faces fascinate us precisely because they are unique, because they stick out of nature and evolution as the most fully developed expression of the pushing of the life force in the intensity of its self-realization. We don't understand why the life force is personalizing in this way, what it is trying to achieve; but we flatly know that it is personalizing because we have our heads and faces as empirical testimony, and as a burden of guilt. We might say that the development of life is life's own burden.

I linger on these ontological thoughts for a very good reason: they tell us what is bothering us deep down. If your face is the most individual part of nature, and if its sticking out is a burden to you because you are an embodiment of the cutting edge of evolution and are no longer safely tucked into the background of nature—if this is so, then it follows that it is dangerous *to have a head*. And I think mankind has always recognized this implicitly, especially on primitive levels of experience. I believe Levin is right when he says that "it is a crime to own a head" in society; historically societies have not tolerated too much individuation, especially on primitive levels. And Levin may even have something when he adds that this is the simplest explanation of head-hunting.[15] Well, there can be no one explanation for the widespread passion for head-hunting;[16] but probably the underlying thing that the various forms of head-taking have in common is that the head is prized as a trophy precisely because it is the most personal part, the one that juts most prominently out of nature. In some sense, too, head-hunting may be a way of projecting onto others one's own guilt for sticking out so much, so that their heads are taken as scapegoats to atone for the guilt. It is as if to say, "*This* will teach *you* to stick out so blatantly." Certainly we feel something of this in societies in which decapitation as punishment was practiced and the heads were publicly displayed. This was a destruction of individuality at its most intensive point, and so a vindication of the pool of faces of the community whose laws had been transgressed. If we extend these thoughts one logical step, we can understand a basic psychoanalytic idea that otherwise seems ridiculous: "in the eyes of culture, to live is a crime."[17] In other words, to live is to stick out, to go beyond safe limits; hence it is to court danger, to be a locus of the possibility of disaster for the group.

If we take all this into view, we should find more palatable to our understanding what Brown meant when he said that social organization was a structure of shared guilt, a symbolic mutual confession of it. Mankind has so many things that put it into a bind that it simply cannot stand them unless it expiates them in some way. Each person cannot stand his own emergence and the many ways in which his organism is dumbly baffled from within and transcended from without. Each person would literally be pulled off his feet and blown away or would gnaw away his own insides with acid anxiety if he did not tuck himself back into something. This is why the main general characteristic of guilt is that it must be shared: man cannot stand alone. And this is precisely what Brown means when he says, "Archaic man gives because he wants to lose; the psychology is . . . self-sacrificial . . . what the giver wants to lose is guilt."[18] Or, metaphorically, "In the gift complex dependence on the mother is acknowledged, and then overcome by mothering others."[19] Society, in other words, is a dramatization of dependence and an exercise in mutual safety by the one animal in evolution who had to figure out a way of appeasing himself as well as nature. We can conclude that primitives were more honest about these things—about guilt and debt— because they were more realistic about man's desperate situation vis-à-vis nature. Primitive man embedded social life in a sacred matrix not necessarily because he was more fearful or masochistic than men in later epochs, but because he saw reality more clearly in some basic ways.[20]

Once we acknowledge this, we have to be careful not to make too much of it; I mean that group living through the motive of guilt is not all humble and self-effacing. As we saw in our consideration of gift giving, not only expiation but the blatant affirmation of power is a primary impetus behind it. If guilt is the experience of fear and powerlessness, then immersing oneself in a group is one way of actively defeating it: groups alone can make big surplus, can generate extravagant power in the form of large harvests, the capture of dangerous animals and many of them, the manufacture of splendid and intricate items based on sophisticated techniques, etc. From the beginning of time the group has represented big power, big victory, much life.

Heroism and Repentance: The Two Sides of Man

If we thus look at both sides of the picture of guilt, we can see that primitive man allocated to himself the two things that man needs most: the experience of prestige and power that constitutes man a hero, and the experience of expiation that relieves him of the guilt of being human. The gift complex took care of both these things superlatively. Man worked for economic surplus of some kind in order to have something to give. In other words, he achieved heroism and expiation at the same time, like the dutiful son who brings home his paper-route earnings and puts them in the family coffer. He protruded out of nature and tucked himself in with the very same gesture, a gesture of heroism–expiation. Man needs self-esteem more than anything; he wants to be a cosmic hero, contributing with his energies to nothing less than the greatness and pleasure of the gods themselves. At the same time this risks inflating him to proportions he cannot stand; he becomes too much like the gods themselves, and he must renounce this dangerous power. Not to do so is to be unbalanced, to run the great sin of *hubris* as the Greeks understood it. *Hubris* means forgetting where the real source of power lies and imagining that it is in oneself.[21]

CHAPTER THREE

The Origin of Inequality

If there is a class which has nothing to lose but its
chains, the chains that bind it are self-imposed,
sacred obligations which appear as objective
realities with all the force of a neurotic delusion.
Norman O. Brown[1]

The origin of inequality among men! This was the question that excited thinkers of the eighteenth century as they combed the globe trying to find humanity in an uncorrupted state. From the early voyages and early anthropology they already saw that primitive society was fairly egalitarian, that compared to the civilized world of that time primitives lived what seemed an unspoiled, undriven sort of life, and one that took very little toll on the world around them. It was the same kind of world that Lévi-Strauss set out to find in the Amazon a couple of centuries later and for which he wrote the same kind of epitaph as the earlier observers had: *A World on the Wane.*[2]

Nobody was very happy with the way history and civilization had turned out, and many thinkers of that time supposed that if the first steps in the process of the oppression of man by man could be pinpointed, then the decay of civilization might be arrested and even reversed. They believed that if man could be shown how he got into his deplorable condition, he would make every intelligent, scientific effort to get out of it. They supposed too that there was nothing naturally evil in man's nature that would prevent him from being able to build a new social world, once he understood the reasons for the mess he was in.

The great Rousseau, with his uncanny intuition of what was significant, began it all with his famous "Discourse on the Origin and Foundations of Inequality among Men" (1755).[3] In that essay he reasoned out how man had gradually fallen from his primitive state of innocence into the conflicts of classes and states. The whole story of the influence of Rousseau's ideas is well known and I am not going to repeat it here. All I want to do is to remind the reader that Rousseau failed to bring about what he hoped for, and so too did the whole tradition which followed him; and I want to sum up why it failed.

The Marxist tradition seized on Rousseau's work because it was exactly what the Marxists needed: the accusation that the state acted tyrannically to hold men in bondage, deprived them of the fruits of their labors, and distributed these fruits mostly among the elite. They attempted to remind society of man's concern for his fellows before the exploitation began and said that once man understood that he had the right to enjoy the fruits of meaningful labor, he would rise up and break the shackles which enslaved him. This was the message of the great Manifesto, the authority for the massive revolutions of this century.

But the great disillusionment of our time is that none of this has led to the liberation of man. Masses of people are still being treated like masses instead of persons, still being sent off like puppets to war, and still slaving all day for purposes they did not fashion or control. In a word, the great revolutions of our time, directed against the state as a structure of domination, have not led to the disappearance of the state, and so they have not led to human equality and freedom.

What went wrong? Obviously something with the plans on the original drawing board; Rousseau's answer to the question posed by the Academy of Dijon was not complete or was beside the mark. We have had to conclude that the question of the origin of inequality among men was not answered by the Marxist tradition. This great historical realization is what prompted the work of the leading school of sociology of our time—the Frankfurt school—a work dedicated to going beyond Marx to a new synthesis: a merger of the materialist and psychological levels of explanation, "the union of Marx and Freud."

If it is not only power and coercion that enslave man, then there must be something in his nature that contributes to his downfall; since this is so, the state is not man's first and only enemy, but he himself harbors an "enemy within." Brown put the problem very well:

We are here at one of the ultimate crossroads in social theory. . . . If the cause of the trouble were force, to "expropriate the expropriators" would be enough. But if force did not establish the domination of the master, then perhaps the slave is somehow in love with his own chains . . . a deeper psychological malady. . . .[4]

Let us review what we know about this "deeper malady." It is a fascinating chapter of psychology in the history of the origins of our inequality.

Curiously, Rousseau himself gave one of the very first psychological explanations in his famous essay. In the famous words which stirred revolutionaries for two centuries he said:

The first person who, having fenced off a plot of ground, took it into his head to say *this is mine* and found people simple enough to believe him, was the true founder of civil society.[5]

In other words, primitive equality was ended by private property, which led to the differential personal ownership of wealth. But the point is that Rousseau doesn't say that the person took the land by *force*, but rather because of something *in the minds* of those around him. As he outlines his theory of the origin of inequality, he places wealth at the last stage and "personal qualities" at the first stage: it is personal qualities that give rise to distinctions of rank and power, and "wealth is the last to which they are reduced in the end."[6] Personal qualities are "the only ones which could attract consideration":

The one who sang or danced the best, the handsomest, the strongest, the most adroit, or the most eloquent became the most highly considered; and that was the first step toward inequality. . . .[7]

It is perhaps an irony of history that one of the very first and most influential tracts of modern revolutionaries, a tract that gave the antistatists their clarion call to end the abuses of expropriation and inequality, *itself rests on the personal, psychological reasons for the very first step in the origin of inequality.* Social imbalances occur because of differences in personal merit and the recognition of that merit by others. Shortly after Rousseau wrote, Adam Ferguson came out with his famous work on social history where he too argued that social inequality was relatively absent on primitive levels because property was comparatively absent.[8] In the most egalitarian primitive societies, those whose economy is based on hunting and gathering, there is no distinction of rank, little or no authority of one individual over another. Possessions are simple and there is no real difference in wealth; property is distributed equally. Yet even on this level individual differences are recognized and already make for real social differentiation. If there is little or no authority to coerce others, there is much room for influence, and influence always stems from personal qualities: extra skill in hunting and warfare, in dealing with the spirits in the invisible world, or simply physical strength and endurance. Old age itself can often have influence. If a person has outlived others, especially when so many die prematurely, he is often thought to have special powers.

Skilled hunters and warriors could actually display these special powers in the form of trophies and ornamental badges of merit. The scalps of the slain enemies and the teeth, feathers, and other ornaments were often loaded with magical power and served as protection. If a man wore a large number of trophies and badges showing how much power he had and how great were his exploits, he became a great mana figure who literally struck terror into the hearts of his enemies.[9] The elaborate decorations of the warrior and hunter were not aimed to make him beautiful, but to show off his skill and courage and so inspired fear and respect. This gave him automatic social distinction; by wearing the tokens of his achievements, the visible memories of his bravery and excellence, he could flaunt his superiority in the eyes of everyone who couldn't make similar displays. The Sioux could announce by certain decorations on his moccassins how many horses he had captured, enemies killed, whether the warrior himself had been wounded, etc.; similar things were conveyed by the feathers he wore and the color they were dyed. Among other tribes, war exploits entitled the warrior to mark himself with certain scarifications and tattoos. Each warrior was literally a walking record of his military campaigns: the "fruit salad" on the chest of today's military men is a direct descendant of this public announcement of "see who I am because of where I have been and what I have done; look how accomplished I am as a death dealer and death defier." It is of course less concrete and living than actual facial and shoulder scars or the carrying of scalps which included the forehead and eyes. But it gives the right to the same kind of proud strutting and social honor and the typical question that the primitive warrior asks: "Who are you that you should talk? Where are your tattoo marks? Whom have you killed that you should speak to me?"[10]

These people, then, are honored and respected or feared, and this is what gives them influence and power. Not only that, it also gives them actual benefits and privileges. Remember that as children we not only deferred to the outstanding boy in the neighborhood but also gave him large chunks of our candy. Primitives who distinguished themselves by personal exploits got the thing that grown men want most—wives. They got them more easily than did others, and often, especially if they were skilled hunters, they took more than one wife. In some cases, too, a noted hunter would claim as his special hunting preserve a piece of land that was common property of the tribe.[11] And so on.

I don't intend to even try to sum up the theoretical details from the vast literature on the growth of hereditary privilege and private accumulation. Besides, there is little agreement on how exactly class society came into existence. There is general agreement on what *pre*class society was, but the process of transformation is shrouded in mystery. Many different factors contributed, and it is impossible to pull them apart and give them their proper weight. Also, the process would not have been uniform or unilinear—the same for all societies in all areas. If we add psychological factors to materialist ones, we must also now add ecological and demographic factors such as population density and scarcity of resources.[12] I don't want to pop my head into the argument among authorities lest it get neatly sliced off. So I would like to sidestep the argument while still remaining focused on what is essential, which, I think must lie in human nature and motives. The most sensitive students of the past 200 years would agree that rank and stratified societies came into being without anyone really noticing; it just "happened," gradually and ineluctably. The vital question, then, it seems to me, is not exactly how it happened but why it was allowed to happen, what there was in human nature that went along so willingly with the process.

The answer to this question seems to me remarkably straightforward. I have said that primitive man recognized differences in talent and merit and already deferred to them somewhat, granted them special privileges. Why? Because obviously these qualities helped to secure life, to assure the perpetuation of the tribe. Exploits in the danger of hunting and war were especially crucial. Why? Because in these activities certain individuals could single themselves out as adept at defying death; the tokens and trophies that they displayed were indications of immortality power or durability power, which is the same thing. If you identified with these persons and followed them, then you got the same immunities they had. This is the basic role and function of the hero in history: he is the one who gambles with his very life and successfully defies death, and men follow him and eventually worship his memory because he embodies the triumph over what they fear most, extinction and death. He becomes the focus of the peculiarly human passion play of the victory over death.

To go back to Rousseau for a moment, we can now see how fanciful the idea is that in the "state of nature" man is free and only becomes unfree later on. Man never was free and cannot be free from his own nature. He carries *within him* the bondage that he needs in order to continue to live. As Rank so well taught us, Rousseau simply did not understand human nature in the round: he "was not able to see that every human being is also equally unfree, that is, we are born in need of authority and we even create out of freedom, a prison. . . ."[13] This insight is the fruit of the outcome of modern psychoanalysis, and there is no going back behind it to the dreams of Rousseau or the utopian revolutionaries. It penetrates to the heart of the human condition and to the principal dynamic of the emergence of historical inequality. We have to say, with Rank, that primitive religion "starts the first class distinction."[14] That is, the individual gives over the aegis of his own life and death to the spirit world; he is already a second-class citizen. The first class distinction, then, was between mortal and immortal, between feeble human powers and special superhuman beings.

Once things started off on this footing, it was only natural that class distinctions should continue to develop from this first impetus: those individuals who embodied supernatural powers, or could somehow plug into them or otherwise use them when the occasion demanded, came to have the same ability to dominate others that was associated with the spirits themselves. The anthropologist Robert Lowie was a specialist on those most egalitarian of all primitive peoples, the Plains Indian tribes. Even these fiercely independent Indians, he tells us, gave up their equalitarian attitudes of everyday life on raiding parties. A Crow Indian would organize a raid only when prompted by his supernatural guardian spirit, and so all those who followed him deferred to him and to his spirit. Again, the overlordship of the invisible world as embodied in certain human personages made temporary slaves of their fellows. No one was more cautious than Lowie about making general statements on primitives, yet when it came to speculating about social evolution he made a very straightforward choice:

I suggest that the awe which surrounded the protégé of supernatural powers formed the psychological basis for more complex political developments. . . . The very same men who flout the pretensions of a fellow-brave grovel before a darling of the gods, render him "implicit obedience and respect."[15]

Power Figures and Power Sources

Primitives were frank about power, and in a spiritual cosmology power is relatively undisguised: it comes from the pool of ancestors and spirits. In our society power resides in technology, and we live and use the artifacts of technology so effortlessly and thoughtlessly that it almost seems we are not beholden to power—until, as said earlier, something goes wrong with an airplane, a generator, a telephone line. Then you see our "religious" anxiety come out.

Power is the life pulse that sustains man in every epoch, and unless the student understands power figures and power sources he can understand nothing vital about social history.

The history of man's "fall" into stratified society can be traced around the figures of his heroes, to whom he is beholden for the power he wants most—to persevere as an organism, to continue experiencing. Again we pick up the thread from the very beginning of our argument and see how intricately it is interwoven in man's career on this planet. If primitive man was not in bondage to the authority of living persons, he at least had some "heroes" somewhere, and these—as said—were the spirit powers, usually of the departed dead, the ancestors. The idea seems very strange to most of us today, but for the primitive it was often the dead who had the most power. In life the individual goes through ritualistic passages to states of higher power and greater importance as a helper of life. For many primitives death is the final promotion to the highest power of all, the passage into the invisible world of the spirits and the ability to use and manipulate the visible world from their new abode.* Many people—and Hocart was one of the foremost of these—have argued that primitives do not fear death as much as we do; but we know that this equanimity is due to the fact that the primitive was usually securely immersed in his particular cultural ideology, which was in essence an ideology of life, of how to continue on and to triumph over death.

It is easy to see the significance of power for the human animal; it is really the basic category of his existence, as the organism's whole world is structured in terms of power. No wonder that Thomas Hobbes could say that man was characterized by "a general inclination, a perpetual and restless desire of power after power, that ceaseth only in death."[16]

One of the first things a child has to learn is how much power

---

* This is not universal among primitives by any means. Some tribes fear the dead for only a little while immediately after death, and then they are thought to become weak. Some tribes fear especially those spirits who represent unfinished and unfulfilled life, spirits of persons who died prematurely and would be envious of the living, and so on. Radin offers a frankly interactionist point of view by saying that the dead are feared because they cannot be controlled as well as when they were alive. P. Radin, *The World of Primitive Man* (New York: Grove Press, 1960), p. 143.

he has and how much exists in others and in the world. Only if he learns this can he be sure of surviving; he has to learn very minutely what powers he can count on to facilitate his life and what powers he has to fear and avoid in order to protect it. So power becomes the basic category of being for which he has, so to speak, a natural respect: if you are wrong about power, you don't get a chance to be right about anything else; and the things that happen when the organism loses its powers are a decrease of vitality and death. Little wonder, then, that primitive man had right away to conceptualize and live according to hierarchies of power and give them his most intense respect. Anthropology discovered that the basic categories of primitive thought are the ideas of mana and taboo, which we can translate simply as "power" and "danger" or "watch out" (because of power). The study of life, people, and the world, then, broke down into an alertness for distributions of power. The more mana you could find to tap, the more taboo you could avoid, the better.

But power is an invisible mystery. It erupts out of nature in storms, volcanoes, meteors, in springtime and newborn babies; and it returns into nature in ashes, winter, and death. The only way we know it is there is to see it in action. And so the idea of mana, or special power erupting from the realm of the invisible and the supernatural, can only be spotted in the unusual, the surpassing, the excellent, that which transcends what is necessary or expected. From the very beginning, the child experiences the awesomeness of life and his problems of survival and well-being in other people; and so persons come to be the most intimate place where one looks to be delighted by the specialness of mysterious life, or where one fears to be overwhelmed by powers that he cannot understand or cope with. It is natural, then, that the most immediate place to look for the eruptions of special power is in the activities and qualities of persons; and so, as we saw, eminence in hunting, extra skill and strength, and special fearlessness in warfare right away marked those who were thought to have an extra charge of power or mana. They earned respect and special privileges and had to be handled gently because they were both an asset and a danger: in their very persons they were an open fount between two worlds, the visible and the invisible, and power passed through them as through an electric circuit.

The most unashamed pretender to supernatural powers was, on the primitive level, the medicine man, or shaman. He invented the specialty of entering into the world of the dead and coming back from it unharmed; he went on these supernatural trips and personally carried out whatever business the tribe or members of it had in the powerful world of the spirits; he went to see a dead soul safely to the other side, to harangue the invisible spirits and make them let go of a sick person, etc. The shaman was the hero who "died" and was reborn unfailingly, who thus regularly acted out man's triumph over death and evil, and who established man's link with the invisible power world. It was an agonizing role to play, and it was played best by those individuals who actually were "seized by spirits" and "killed" by them—the epileptics.[17] Nothing strikes greater terror into man's heart than to witness an eruption of power from the depths of nature that he cannot understand or control—whether it is lava erupting from a volcano or the foam and convulsions of an epileptic. And so for all these reasons primitive man saw the epileptic shaman as a natural hero, a source of fear and respect.* The shaman was the mystifier *par excellence*, and it was only logical that he should often be more powerful than chiefs, more feared, and get greater rewards. Sometimes he allied himself with the chief of a tribe, and the resulting exploitation was what Radin called "clearly a form of gangsterism."[18]

Radin's writings on the origins of inequality are the most sensitively probing and ruthless that I know. In his view primitive society was from the very beginning a struggle by individuals and groups for special privileges—who would get the best meat, the easiest access to women, some leisure and security. The elders always tried to arrange these for their own benefit, and so did the shamans. On the simplest levels of culture they were already organizing themselves into an exclusive fraternity so as to get and keep maximum power. How does one get maximum power in a cosmology where ritual is the technics that manufactures life? Ob-

---

* He was also the first natural systematizer of religion because he actually had experiences of rebirth, reincarnation, and eternal life in the dream state following a convulsive seizure. These experiences are more or less characteristic for all epileptics. This is how we understand the birth of these basic religious notions, verified "objectively" by many individuals. Cf. W. Bromberg and P. Schilder, "The Attitude of Psychoneurotics toward Death," *Psychoanalytic Review*, 1936, 23:21–22.

viously by getting control of the formulas for the technics. Very early the elders and the religious personages tried to get control of the ritual. In his brilliant chapter "The Crises of Life and Their Rituals"[19] Radin argues that the religious systematizer built his symbolic interpretations around the crises of life, those passages where one's identity was in doubt, where he was moving from one state to another, where everything had to go smoothly in order for a flowering out or birth into a new status to take place. And so the puberty and the death rituals came to be surrounded by the greatest importance, wherein lay the greatest possibilities of bungling. Radin makes the fascinating point that over and beyond the frankly religious and psychological nature of these passages, there is a social-economic purpose to them—or rather to the control of them by certain groups. Talking about puberty rites of the Australian aborigines he says:

. . . over and above all other reasons is the somewhat cynically expressed purpose of the old men of having novices supply them, for many years, with regular presents in the form of animal food, of reserving the choice dishes for themselves by the utilization of the numerous food taboos imposed on the younger people, and, finally, of keeping the young women for themselves.

And again, with another tribe, Radin observes that "the fundamental and immediate objective was to maintain power in the hands of the older people and to keep the women in proper subjection." Those who systematized the puberty, he concludes, weren't obeying some mystical, myth-making urge in the unconscious.

Rather . . . specific individuals banded together formally or informally, individuals who possess a marked capacity for articulating their ideas and for organizing them into coherent systems, which, naturally, would be of profit to them and to those with whom they are allied.[20]

I linger on Radin's views for a good reason. They put closure on the very beginnings of the modern debate on the origins of inequality. Adam Ferguson had argued that the primitive world had to break up because of man's burning ambition to improve himself, to compete and stand out in a ceaseless struggle for perfection.[21]

Ferguson's was a very straightforward and unburdened view of man. As we would put it, the frail human creature tries to change his position from one of insignificance in the face of nature to one of central importance; from one of inability to cope with the overwhelming world to one of absolute control and mastery of nature. Each organism is in a struggle for more life and tries to expand and aggrandize itself as much as possible. And the most immediate way to do this is in one's immediate social situation—vis-à-vis others. This is what Hobbes meant with his famous observation that evil is a robust child. Rousseau quoted this in his essay on inequality, and his whole intent was to show that this isn't true, that the child is innocent and does evil in a number of clumsy and unintentional ways. But this is just what Hobbes was driving at, that the organism expands itself in the ways open to it and that this has destructive consequences for the world around it. Rousseau and Hobbes were right, evil is "neutral" in origin, it derives from organismic robustness—but its consequences are real and painful.

What Radin did was to bring all this up to date with an acute understanding of personality types and interpersonal dynamics and a frankly materialistic perspective on society. This is already the makings of a union of Marx and Freud. Seen in this way, social life is the saga of the working out of one's problems and ambitions on others. What else could it be, what else are human objects for? I think it is along lines such as these that we would find the psychological dynamics for a sophisticated Marxist philosophy of history; it would be based on power, but it would include individual deviance and interpersonal psychology, and it would reflect a "social contract" forged in desire and fear. The central question of such a sophisticated Marxist philosophy of history would be, Who has the power to mystify, how did he get it, and how does he keep it? We can see how naive the traditional Marxist view of simple coercion is: it doesn't begin to take into account what we must now call *the sacredness of class distinctions*. There is no other accurate way to speak. What began in religion remains religious. All power is, as Brown says, sacred power, because it begins in the hunger for immortality; and it ends in the absolute subjection to people and things which represent immortality power.

And so Brown could offer his own biting criticism of Rousseau:

If the emergence of social privilege marks the Fall of Man, the Fall took place not in the transition from "primitive communism" to "private property" but in the transition from ape to man.[22]

That is, from a type of animal that had no notion of the sacred to one that did. And if sacredness is embodied in persons, then they dominate by a psychological spell, not by physical coercion. As Brown puts it, "Privilege is prestige, and prestige in its fundamental nature as in the etymology of the word, means deception and enchantment."[23] Thus Brown could conclude—in the epigraph we have borrowed for this chapter—that the chains that bind men are self-imposed.

If we left this idea unadorned, it would still need explaining: why are men so *eager* to be mystified, so *willing* to be bound in chains? The bind is explained by one idea, the truly great idea that emerged from psychoanalysis and that goes right to the heart of the human condition: the phenomenon of *transference.**

People take the overwhelmingness of creation and their own fears and desires and project them in the form of intense mana onto certain figures to which they then defer. They follow these figures with passion and with a trembling heart. When one thinks of his own eager fascinations, he can feel revolted by himself and by the obedient throngs who look with such timidity and satisfaction on the "leader." Look how the girls blush, how hands reach out tremblingly, how eyes lower and dart to one side, how quickly a few choke up, ready for tearful and grateful submission, how smugly those nearest to the leader smile, how puffed up they walk— how the Devil himself seems to have contrived an instant, mass puppet show with real live creatures. But there is no way of avoiding the fatality of it: the thousands of hearts palpitating, the gallons of adrenalin, of blood rushing to the cheeks—it is all lived truth, an animal's reaction to the majesty of creation. If anything is false about it, it is the fact that thousands of human forms feel inferior and beholden to an identical, single human form.

In all this I am not negating the pure Marxian side of historical

* For a more detailed examination of the nature of transference please see my extensive summary in chap. 7 of *The Denial of Death* (New York: The Free Press, 1973).

domination; that is real enough and we know it. But there can never be a way of relieving or eliminating the domination of structures of power without coming to grips with the spell of power, a spell that explains voluntary self-alienation whether it deals with spirits or with Soviets. Men are literally hypnotized by life and by those who represent life to them, which explains the passion of submission that Melville summed up so brilliantly in *Moby Dick,* in the quarterdeck scene when Ahab consecrates the harpoons. In other words, Marxism has to come to grips with the conservative argument: that there is something in human nature that invites inequality no matter what we do. One recent writer calls this "functional inequality," and sees it as a completely neutral and unavoidable factor in social life.[24] Or, as I would say with Rank, men are "fate-creating" agents: they coerce by simply existing; they do not even necessarily, like Ahab, try to project electric mana; they are already a natural vortex of the problems of life. We can sum all this up in one sentence that presents to narrow Marxism the most fundamental challenge it has faced: *men fashion unfreedom as a bribe for self-perpetuation.* What is the shape of a revolutionary philosophy of history that would begin to take full account of that?

The Evolution of Inequality

Radin's view of how shamans and elders gained control of ritual is full of volition, scheming, competitiveness; the more shrewd, introverted, selfish members of the tribe outwitted and outplayed the more plodding and guileless, the ones who carried the burden of the tribe's work.[1] At the level of equalitarian society—simple hunting and gathering tribes—Radin's scheme of the growth of privilege through the deliberate creation of mystique is compelling. But what I like about Hocart's view of the growth of privilege at a later stage of social evolution is that it accents the other side: *the common accord with which men reach for their own subjection.*

In Radin's equalitarian society organismic well-being is achieved by an economy of reciprocal exchange; goods are freely traded among the tribe. In Hocart's rank society there is a new economic process: the flow of goods funnels to a center of power—an authoritarian figure—who receives the fruits of everyone's labor and redistributes those fruits; he can order people to work on his behalf or on someone else's, and he takes the surplus, pools it, and then gives it out as needed.[2]

Immediately the question arises, Why did people go from an economy of simple sharing among equals to one of pooling via an authority figure who has a high rank and absolute power? The answer is that *man wanted a visible god always present to receive his offerings, and for this he was willing to pay the price of his own subjection.* In Hocart's words:

The Fijians had invisible gods, sometimes present in the priest or in an animal; they preferred a god always present, one they could see and speak to, and the chief was such a god. That is the true reason for a Fijian chief's existence: he receives the offerings of his people, and in consequence they prosper.[3]

That is, they prosper *because* there is a god right on the spot that visibly accepts their offerings; thus there is no doubt about their favor in his eyes.

So great was the belief that a visible god meant prosperity that chiefless tribes were eager to get a chief "as soon as they could find a nobleman whose high rank or age gave hopes that he would be acceptable to the spirits."[4] Prosperity and chiefs were associated because the tribes with great chiefs were actually more prosperous. Hocart explains this as a circular process: the wealthier tribes were more energetic, and so they rose among their neighbors. But part of the reason that they were more energetic was that "there is no doubt that present divinity evoked an enthusiasm which acted as a tonic, and braced men to greater efforts." "A Fijian will put his back into his work when striving to shine in the eyes of the great man."[5] Imagine what a stimulus it would be to our own efforts today if we could actually see that God was satisfied with the fruits of our labors. Again we come back to the natural genius of primitive man, who provided himself with what man needs most: to *know daily* that he is living right in the eyes of God, that his workaday action has cosmic value—no, even that it enhances God Himself!

Men lean on increase and creation ritual especially when times are bad; it is then that their spiritual technology has to work. So if they got along without a king in good times, they would want one when times got bad. Besides, says Hocart, if you are without a king you are in a position of inferiority in relation to your neighbors; when others parade their visible god, and their favor in his eyes, how can you stand being shown up as having no god of your own? The Jews were mocked in the ancient world because they had no image of their god, he seemed like a mere figment of their imagination; next to the visible splendor of the Pharaoh, the God of Israel seemed like a phantom of a deluded mind. Most of all, one always knew how one stood with the visible god, but the Israelis were never sure how they stood with their invisible one— the whole thing must have seemed sick.

To speak of the Pharaoh is to sum up the whole process: once you have a visible ritual principal in the form of a chief or a king, a visible god, by definition you already have divine kingship—the great emergent tyranny of the ancient world. And we can see in one swoop why ancient man so willingly embraced his new alienated status under divine kingships, as the chiefless tribes of Fiji eagerly chose a chief with all the troubles this meant. It all goes back to our discussion in Chapter One about macro- and microcosmization, processes whereby man entwined his own destiny with that of the cosmos by bringing the heavens into human affairs and by blowing himself up as the center of concern of the universe. We also saw that ritual was an enactment of the struggle between the forces of light and life and those of darkness and death. With the technique of ritual offerings man sought to bring the invisible powers of nature to bear on his visible well-being. Well, the divine king sums up this whole cosmology all in himself. He is the god who receives offerings, the protagonist of light against dark, and the embodiment of the invisible forces of nature—specifically, the sun. In Hocart's happy phrase, he is the "Sun-Man." Divine kingship sums up the double process of macro- and microcosmization: it represents a "solarization of man, and a humanizing of the sun."[6]

For early man the emanations of light and heat from the sun were the archetypes of all miraculous power: the sun shines from afar and by its invisible touch causes life to unfold and expand.[7] We can't say much more about this mystery even today. Hocart asks whether ancient man was altogether wrong in his main conception "that animal or vegetable energy on this earth is after all little else than bottled sunshine?" And once man made the equation king equals sun, was he altogether wrong to believe that "this bottled sunshine manifests itself again in other forms of action at a distance by look and by voice? After all, man does act at a distance by means of the light and sound waves that emanate from him."[8] The point is, concludes Hocart, that once you admit that a man can become one with the sun, it follows that the actions of the one are the actions of the other, that the king himself in his person, will vivify the earth. When the Pharaoh's name was mentioned, it was followed by the words "life," "prosperity," "health"![9] In these three words are summed up the timeless and universal hunger of men. And when they had made that most wonderful invention of all, a living embodiment of prosperity, a Sun-Man, how expect them not to fall into eager thralldom? I use the word "invention" advisedly: the individual Sun-Man was the focus of a cosmology of invisible energy, like the modern computer and atomic reactor, and he aroused the same hopes and yearning they arouse for the perfectly ordered, plentifully supplied life. Like the reactor, too, he reflected back energy-power on those around him: just the right amount and they prospered; too much and they withered into decay and death.

At this point we might be tempted to get up on our high horse and proclaim that the simple fact is that the atomic theory of power is true, and the Sun-Man theory false. But we have to remind ourselves, soberly, that we haven't quite abandoned the earlier theory; it still holds a fascination for us and we still live in large measure by its compellingness. We know about the genuine mana that surrounds presidents and prime ministers: look at Churchill and the whole Kennedy family; in true primitive style each member of the family is interchangeable because each partakes of the same kin pool of power. And in those "least superstitious" and "most humanistic and scientific" states of Russia and China, witness the aura of mana that surrounds their chairmen. Caesar could not have hoped for more. The political leader only becomes suspect when it is thought that he has no special powers, or has lost them. Then, after the manner of the ancient chiefs and kings, he is quickly "done away with" by a vote or a coup in favor of a new power symbol. As the ancients believed that the kingdom would perish if the king's mana ebbed, so do we feel uncomfortable and anxious if the figure "at the top" doesn't show real excellence, some kind of "magic."

The identification of the mana figure with one's own well-being still influences too the democratic voting process: just as in traditional society, we tend to vote for the person who already represents health, wealth, and success so that some of it will rub off on us. Whence the old adage "Nothing succeeds like success." This attraction is also especially strong in certain religious cults of the Father Divine type: the followers want to see wealth flaunted in the person of their leader, hoping that some of it will radiate back to them. This is a direct continuation of the tradition of weighing the Aga Khan in diamonds.[10]

The Centralization of Ritual

Once men consented to live by the redistribution of life's goods through a god figure who represented life, they had sealed their fate. There was no stopping the process of the monopolization of life in the king's hands. It went like this: The king of ritual principal was in charge of the sacred objects of the group and had to hold the prescribed ceremonies by a strict observance of the customs of the ancestors. This made him a repository of custom, an authority on custom. "Custom" is a weak word in English to convey something really momentous, as we saw; custom is the abstruse technical lore that runs the machinery for the renewal of nature. It is the physics, medicine, and mechanics of primitive society. Imagine our trying to fight a plague with faulty chemicals, and you can understand that custom equals life. The authority on custom, then, is the supreme regulator of certain departments of nature. But this regulation is so useful to the tribe—in fact it is life itself—that it naturally comes to be extended to all departments. Again, I think an analogy to modern life may convey some of the flavor: what first began as the miraculous harnessing of electric power in the electric bulb now extends to toothbrushes, razors, garden tools, typewriters, etc. What was at first limited to ritual and to the seat of ritual gradually spread "to the whole of the king's realm and the whole life of his subjects."[11] After all, if you are going to be supreme regulator of the world, it is only logical that you should gradually encompass the whole world. If your invisible mechanics works in one area, there is no reason why it should not work in another, you have only to try it. And you try it by extending your ritual prerogative to cover the case: you extend the veil of your mana power over wider and wider jurisdictions. It seems like a benign and harmless enough process, one you might never even notice and in fact might want to happen—but what is happening is the complete entrenchment of social inequality. Hocart sums it up in a nutshell:

Fijian chiefs were great sticklers for etiquette. They were quick to resent offences against their dignity and unseemly behaviour in their precincts. . . . These may seem petty matters; but they are fraught with great possibilities. The Fijian chief has only to extend his precincts and interpret widely the traditional rules of ceremonial behaviour in order to acquire a criminal jurisdiction, and increase his interference with the life of his subjects. . . . By sanctifying anything they [the chiefs in Polynesia] brought it within the sphere of ritual, that is their own sphere. This was certainly not done suddenly, but by persistently extending the applications of taboo [sacred power], as we shall see our English kings extend their peace.[12]

You can see that the whole force of social sanction would fall behind the king to protect his definitions of social custom and his ritual prerogatives; otherwise the tribe would lose well-being and life. We might say that the safeguarding of custom imposes tyranny because of the need for the king's power. The more successful a king, the more prerogatives he could enjoy: he was judged by results. "If the harvests were good the people were prepared to put up with a moderate amount of tyranny."[13]

Protection of custom and criminal jurisdiction go together so naturally, then, that we should not wonder that ritual centraliza tion also came to mean control of the power to punish. Another large step in the evolution of inequality seems to me to be summed up here. To us a police force is a part of life, as inevitable, it seems, as death and taxes; we rely on the police to punish those who hurt us. But it hasn't always been so. In simple egalitarian societies there is no police force, no way to settle a wrong except to do so yourself, family against family. But if there is no police force to enforce the law, there is also none to coerce you for any reason. You have to stay alert, but you are also freer. A police force is usually drawn up temporarily for special occasions and then disbanded. Among the Plains Indians, for example, these special occasions were the buffalo hunt, mass migrations, war parties, and major festivals; it was then that the police had to maintain order and harmonize and synchronize activities so as to ensure a maximum buffalo kill, etc. At these times the police force enjoyed absolute authority, even the power of life and death; and yet among the Plains Indians this foundation for autocracy never hardened into permanent form.

Theorists of social evolution have given much attention to the police function in egalitarian societies and have speculated on why it didn't develop into a permanent coercive structure, a stratified state of the modern type.[14] The answer seems to be that the entrenchment of a police force or even a military organization is not all by itself the road to institutionalized inequality. Offhand you might think that blatant power would exercise its own fascination and its own irresistible coercion, but in the affairs of men things don't seem to work that way: men will not give in to power unless it is accompanied by mystification, as in the service of something that has a grander aura of legitimacy, of symbolic compellingness. So Lowie concluded that the religious figures command more respect than the military ones, and Fried thinks that the emergence of the economics of redistribution is much more significant than military organizations.[15] In other words, men seem first to have allowed or even welcomed the ascendancy over them of visible gods; after that, to accept punishment from the agents of these gods is a natural and logical step.

But the result, alas, is not as innocent as it must have seemed to people living during these transitions. What they were doing was bartering away social equality and a measure of personal independence for prosperity and order. There was now nothing to stop the state from taking more and more functions and prerogatives into itself, from developing a class of special beings at the center and inferior ones around it, or from beginning to give these special beings a larger share of the good things of the earth.* Not only of the earth, but also of afterlife: evidently the common people of Tonga had no souls, and Hocart believes that the lower classes of society did not get souls until they imitated the ceremonies of the king.

Once you went from an economy of simple sharing to one of redistribution, goods gradually ceased to be your natural right. Again a logical, almost forced development. How this actually came about is shrouded in the depths of prehistory, and it must have been a long and varied development; we can't trace it except for hints here and there, but we can empirically compare tribal life

---

* This is one of Hocart's major arguments throughout all his studies, that the whole of archaic society set itself up to imitate the divine cosmos of the king, and that we can still see vestiges of this organization. His exploration is a fascinating one and opens up a whole new vista to the student, whether Hocart proves to be describing a universally true phenomenon or not (cf. K, pp. 235, 156).

with later stages of social evolution. What we see is that private interests became more and more separated from public interests—until today we hardly know what a public interest is.

Students who look for the point at which economic activity and social morality begin to pull apart usually focus on the potlatch: it was evidently around the process of redistribution that gift giving gradually changed into grabbing and keeping. As the power figures got more and more ascendancy vis-à-vis the group, they could take a fixed portion of the surplus with less involvement in the life of the people. The classic potlatch, as practiced, say, among the Kwakiutl, was a redistribution ceremonial pure and simple. It embraced the twin urges talked about in Chapter Two, heroism and expiation. The more goods one could amass and give away, the greater a coup of oneupmanship one pulled off, the more power one could generate, the bigger the personal victory. The object was to humiliate rivals, to stand out as tall as possible as a big man, a hero. At the same time, the grander was the expiation before the community and the gods to whom the goods were offered. Both the individual urge to maximum self-feeling and the community well-being were served. But this classic social ceremonial had to change with the gradual development of hereditary privilege, so that the chiefs became the principal takers and destroyers of goods. In this way a feudal structure could naturally develop.[16]

Another suggestive way of looking at this development is to see it as a shift of the balance of power, away from a dependence on the invisible world of the gods to a flaunting of the visible world of things. Again, it is only natural that once the god became visible in the person of the king, his powers became those of this world—visible, temporal powers in place of invisible, eternal ones. He would come to measure his power by the piles of things he actually possessed, by the glory of his person, and not, as before, by the efficiency of the ritual technics for the renewal of nature.

This represents a basic change in man's whole stance toward the world, from a partnership with animal spirits, a sharer in nature's bounty, to a big boss, a darling of the gods. Hocart calls it the "growing conceit" of man, and we know that this *hubris* comes directly from a belief that one's own powers are more important than anything else. In the old totemic world picture individuals did not stand out as much. There was belief in the fusion of human and animal spirits, a kind of spiritual unification of the life of the tribe with a sector of nature. Out of the invisible world of spirits life tumbled in an endless cycle of embodiments and returns. The individual got his sense of self-expansion and protection by sharing in the collectivity of social and animal souls, in the clan and its totems. I don't want to get tied up in an argument with modern anthropology about what exactly totemism is or isn't, or even, as Lévi-Strauss questioned, whether it existed or not. What is certain is that spirit beliefs permeated primitive society and with them the sense of some kind of mystical participation with animals and nature, a participation for the purposes of the control and renewal of life. The individual got a sense of organismic durability by identifying with the fund of ancestral spirits. What also seems certain is that the entire community functioned as a kind of regenerative priesthood, as each member had a share in the ritual.*

The shared communal ritual recedes before the chief or king as he comes to control and centralize it in his person. The "conceit" comes in when he himself becomes the guarantee of life and it is no longer the group as a whole. We might put it this way: in the classic potlatch the accumulation of visible power was certainly there in the piles of goods, and it was very compelling and meant to be so, but it had not yet taken the ascendancy over the group, had not yet upset the shared dependence, the reliance on gods and spirits, animals and ancestors. But with the historical detachment

---

* This step in social evolution raises some fascinating questions about the basic nature of man and his attitudes toward the world around him. Often these days we tend to romanticize about how primitives "naturally" respected nature and animal life and handled them gently and reverently. Certainly this was often true, but we also know that primitives could be very casual and even cruel with animals. Hocart throws an interesting light on this by pointing out that once man got enough power over the world to forgo the old totemic ritual identifications, he became more and more eager to disclaim any relationship with animals. Hence the eclipse of animal identification historically. We know that primitives *used* animals in the ritual technics, but Hocart says this doesn't mean that they always revered them or that respect was the primary thing: the primary thing was identification for use. This would explain why, once man got more secure control over the visible world, he found it easy to dissociate himself entirely from animals. Otto Rank has discussed brilliantly the change from Egyptian to Greek art as the gradual defeat of the animal by the spiritual principle, the climax of a long struggle by man to liberate himself from his animal nature. See Hocart, K, p. 146, KC, pp. 53–54, SO, p. 35; and Rank, *Art and Artist* (New York: Knopf, 1932), pp. 356 ff.

of power figures into feudal structures, the generation of wealth as moral power for the community became a caricature. Nowhere is this better seen than in the ancient world: the "potlatch" practiced by the Romans was a perfect example of the degeneration of the primitive gift complex. The emperors "gave" huge public entertainments in the arenas, public buildings, and monuments, whose walls were duly inscribed, as is the Pantheon in Rome, with the name of the giver. But we know that these givers amassed and passed on more than they gave; their gifts were only a sop to the community, more public relations than expiation; they gave to the eyes of men and not to the gods. We see the final evolution of this empty potlatch practiced in the western world, our cities, parks, and universities carrying buildings with the names Carnegie, Rockefeller, Hearst, Macmillan-Bloedel—men who grabbed millions from the labor and lands of others and offered back to the public a pittance. It was good public relations for alienated masses who understood nothing, but it was hardly expiation for public guilt; it was almost all proud heroism, the flaunting of power with very little mixture of repentance.

Conclusion: The Eclipse of Communal Ritual

Most people would agree that the word "alienation" applies to modern man, that something happened in history which gradually despoiled the average man, transformed him from an active, creative being into the pathetic consumer who smiles proudly from our billboards that his armpits are odor-free around the clock. The main task of historical Marxism was to loudly proclaim this "downfall" of man; and thinkers as diverse as Whitehead, Kierkegaard, and Trotsky agreed. This is still the truth at the heart of the myth of the "noble savage," and part of the reason that Rousseau's thought is still not dead. Historical man lost something that early man had. It would take volumes to talk about the many dimensions of historical alienation, and the subject has been covered in the most complex ways. But there is a suggestive way of looking at the problem that cuts right to the heart of it, and that is from the two angles we have been using here: first, to say that man changed from a privileged sharer of goods to someone who was dependent on the redistribution of goods; and second, to say that he was gradually dispossessed of the most intimate creative role he had ever invented, that of a practitioner of ritual.

The family or clan is a ritual unit, which makes each person a member of a priesthood. Often each clan has a specific function in the regeneration of nature, its own ceremonial lodge, sacred fire, ritual songs, and ceremonies which belong to it alone. It is easy enough for us to talk about a household that has its own cult and sacred fire, but can we imagine what it means to step into a hut that has a sacred fire, a hut filled with technologists who know the secret ways of rejuvenating earthly life? I have already talked about what this did for the individual as a cosmic hero, but it bears repeating again and again because I don't think we can easily get the feel of the thing or understand what is missing when it is lost. And historically, precisely what happened is that it was lost. Family ritual was absorbed into state ritual. Hocart sums this whole development up in a few trenchant lines:

The great difference between our society and *most* non-European societies is that the national ritual, of which the Pope or the sovereign [president, chairman, prime minister, etc.] is the head, has swallowed up all others. Hence the clan and all other ritual organizations have disappeared. . . . The disappearance of the intermediate groupings has left the married couple face to face with the state.[17]

But now a married couple, completely shorn of sacred status, does not live in a sacred house, belong to a holy clan, or possess the secret technology for the renewal of nature. Which means that it is face to face with the state but with no real *powers* of its own. As the modern married couple does not understand the high estate from which it has fallen historically, it can be quite content to regenerate nature in the person of a child and to renovate prosperity by working in a factory. Needless to say, these are activities for the promotion of life which have quite different qualities and intensities, and one of the great lessons historical psychology can teach is what new ways man has had to invent for the pursuit of life after the disappearance of the primitive world picture.

CHAPTER FIVE

The New Historical Forms of Immortality Power

History in itself is nothing but applied psychology.
Hence we must look to theoretical psychology to
give us the clew to its true interpretation.
Karl Lamprecht[1]

We can now take a step that we prepared for in the Introduction. There, remember, we saw that man wants what all organisms want: continuing experience, self-perpetuation as a living being. But we also saw that man—alone among all other organisms—had a consciousness that his life came to an end here on earth, and so he had to devise another way to continue his self-perpetuation, a way of transcending the world of flesh and blood, which was a perishable one. This he did by fixing on a world which was not perishable, by devising an "invisible-project" that would assure his immortality in a spiritual rather than physical way.

This way of looking at the doings of men gives a direct key to the unlocking of history. We can see that what people want in any epoch is a way of transcending their physical fate, they want to guarantee some kind of indefinite duration, and culture provides them with the necessary immortality symbols or ideologies; societies can be seen as structures of immortality power.

Two of the most brilliant and economical orderings of history from this point of view, to my mind, are those of Otto Rank and Norman O. Brown. Their work gave us a grip on the manifold of historical fact from an intimate psychological point of view—something scholars had been seeking since the nineteenth century without success. In this chapter I want to take up Rank's work, which in fact came a full generation before the work of Brown. Brown; he

63

swept over the whole panorama of social-evolutionary thought and the mass of scholarly monographs on the primitive world and early history; this was a mountain of scholarly insight from several disciplines that was so sprawling and technical that little general sense could be made out of it. Rank pulled it all together with a single principle, what we might call the principle of immortality striving. It was a universal principle firmly anchored in each individual person, no matter who he was; it was present in each culture, no matter how varied its beliefs might seem, or how much mankind itself seemed to change from epoch to epoch. Beliefs were not fixed and final realities; they varied from period to period, from one social form to another. What was fixed was the principle of a "dominant immortality-ideology." In each historical period or social group, man thought that he lived absolute truth because his social life gave expression to his deepest innate hunger. And so Rank could say, "Every conflict over truth is in the last analysis just the same old struggle over . . . immortality."[2] If anyone doubts this, let him try to explain in any other way the life-and-death viciousness of all ideological disputes. Each person nourishes his immortality in the ideology of self-perpetuation to which he gives his allegiance; this gives his life the only abiding significance it can have. No wonder men go into a rage over fine points of belief: if your adversary wins the argument about truth, *you die.* Your immortality system has been shown to be fallible, your life becomes fallible. History, then, can be understood as the succession of ideologies that console for death. Or, more momentously, *all* cultural forms are *in essence sacred* because they seek the perpetuation and redemption of the individual life. This is the breathtaking import of Rank's attempt to see history as stages or successions of immortality ideologies. Culture *means* that which is super*natural;* all culture has the basic mandate to transcend the physical, to permanently transcend it. All human ideologies, then, are affairs that deal directly with *the sacredness of the individual or the group life,* whether it seems that way or not, whether they admit it or not, whether the person knows it himself or not.

What does history look like viewed from this angle? We already have seen what the primitive world looked like. As both Rank and Brown saw it, what characterized "archaic" man was that he attained immortality "by assimilation into the fund of ancestral souls, out of which comes each generation and into which they return."[3] This eternal cycle of rebirth was self-renewing if helped with the proper communal rituals. The group, then, guaranteed its own self-perpetuation. Its duty was to strengthen the life force by fulfilling ritual obligations. The group alone conferred immortality —which is why the individual immersed himself so completely in its ideology, and why duty took precedence over everything else. Only in this way can we understand the willing self-denials of man in society; he accepts the social limitations on his appetites because the group gives expression to the most important appetite of all, the hunger for the continuation of life. Why would human beings put infants through the torture of lip plugs, subject themselves to circumcisions and repeated subincisions, perforated nasal septums, neck rings, holes in the tongue, torn flesh, joints, muscles— why would they even willingly die—if not for the ultimate stake: immortality, the triumph over the extinction of the body and its insignificance.

And so Rank and Brown could argue that from the beginning of society and prehistory man has repressed himself, tamed himself, in a barter for greater power and durability. And the record of the taming of man is found in the "immortality symbols" that men have used and discarded across the face of history. Unlike Freud, Rank argued that all taboos, morals, customs, and laws represent a self-limitation of man so that he could transcend his condition, get more life by denying life. As he paradoxically put it, men seek to preserve their immortality rather than their lives. This way of looking at society represents a fundamental revision of Freud in the very central pillar of Freud's system: the theory of sex, the idea that the primary aim of man is pleasure, the gratification of erotic drives. Freud said that man gives these drives up only grudgingly to society, and then only because he is forced to by superior authority and power. Rank, on the other hand, said that sexual restrictions "from the first" were "voluntary, spontaneous" acts, not the result of external authority.[4] And the reason was that man was from the first willing to barter his body for higher spiritual values, for more life; or, as we would put it technically, the body was the first thing that one abandoned for the project of cultural immortality, and it was abandoned, not because of fear of the fathers, but ironically because of love of life. Besides, if the individual is willing to renounce life, to shrink back from it in order to persevere, then he would also need society to map out safe sexuality for him. Rank makes the same quasi-cynical observation on this as Durkheim had: primitive social organization did not so much restrict the individual sexually as actually make it possible for him to have the sexual life that "he had always been neurotically ready to sacrifice for the sake of his personal immortality.[5]

We already have seen, with Hocart, how willingly primitive man embraced the institution of kingship because it was equated with prosperity; from the beginning men renounced some dimensions of life in order to open up others, and this is what made it easy for monolithic historical structures of power to take shape and to choke out life still more. All that these new structures had to do was to promise the same immortality, only now in different forms.

The Family and the State, or the "Sexual Era"

With the discovery of agriculture began the breakup of the primitive world, the rise of the early states; and now social organization came to be focused in the patriarchal family under the state's legal protection. It was at this time that biological fatherhood became of dominant importance because it became the universal way of assuring personal immortality.[6] Rank called this the "sexual era" because physical paternity was fully recognized as the royal road to self-perpetuation via one's children—in fact, it was one's bounden duty. The institution of marriage extended from the king to his people, and every father became a kind of king in his own right, and his home a castle. Under Roman law the father had tyrannical rights over his family; he ruled over it legally; as Rank was quick to observe, *famulus* equals servant, slave.[7] In the primitive world, we might say, the child had been the bearer of the *collective* immortality, since it was through him that the souls of the ancestors reentered the world. This is one reason why many primitives handled their children so gently: the child was actually in the process of giving birth to himself with the help of the ancestral spirit; if one was mean to him, the spirit might be upset and with-draw from this world.

Under the ideology of the patriarchal family, the child becomes the *individual* successor to his father—actually, then, *merely the son* of a father, and is no longer the independent mediator of spirits from the ancestral world. But this is now the only spiritual lineage in which the son can perpetuate himself in turn.[8] This is why, too, fathers could be despotic with their children: they were merely objects to whom one had oneself given life. Today we are shocked when we read of the ancient Greek who blinded his sons for dis-obeying him and going off to war—but their lives were literally his personal property, and he had this authority and used it.

What is of great interest in this development is the intimate unity of patriarchal family ideology with that of kingship. The king represented the new fountainhead of spiritual power in which the subjects were nourished. In primitive society the entire group had created magical power by means of the jointly celebrated ritual. But with the gradual development of specialized ritualists and priests, the *power to create power* often fell to a special class and was no longer the possession of the whole collectivity. Where this happened it helped to turn the average man into an impotent subject. In many agrarian societies the priests went on to develop astronomy, calen-dars, and rituals of power for the control of nature via magic, whereas previously each person had helped exercise such control via the communal rituals. Without the priests' calendar, how would the farmer know the auspicious days for planting? With their astronomy the priests accrued the tremendous prestige of predicting eclipses; and then they exercised the fantastic power of bringing back the sun out of the clutches of darkness. Not only did they save the world from chaos in such ways, but in some places (e.g., India) they possessed the secret ritual for the creation of the king's power. Often the kings and priests were solidly allied in a structure of domination that monopolized all sacred power; this completed the development from the tribal level where the shaman would sometimes ally with the chief. All the poor subject could do in these societies was to grovel to the king and bring food to the priests in order to get a mite of magical protective power. The fathers imitated the kings so as to reenact the divine plan in their own homes; in this way they got a reflection of the king's powers.

As Confucian thought had it, if the gentlemen observed proper ritual behavior, the kingdom would flourish. So long as everyone in the kingdom copied the king, fathered sons, married off daughters, kept order in the family, and observed the household rituals, the balance of nature would not be upset in the "divine household."

All this took place in the divine cities, which themselves were eternal, connected to heaven (Babylon equals Gate of the Gods), and protected and regenerated by the priestly rituals. Each city with its pyramidal temples and towers rose like a spire to penetrate the sky, the dimensions of invisible power, and to bathe itself in it. We can still feel this in the Gothic cathedral which penetrated heaven and was bathed in the light and powers of heaven. Rome is called "the eternal city" not because today tourists can always go back and find her as she was when they first visited her a few decades ago, but because she was regenerated in ancient times by centennial rituals, and was thought to have so much power sustaining her that she would never falter. One of the strong impetuses to the triumph of Christianity was the increasing sackings of Rome by the barbarians, which showed everyone that something was wrong with the old powers and some new magical sources had to be tapped.

The divine king in the sacred city bathing the holy empire— these were a power tool in which the fathers nourished themselves while they assured their own perpetuation in the person of their sons. We can see that this represents a new kind of unification experience, with a focal point of power, that in its own way tries to recapture the intense unity of primitive society, with its focus of power in the clan and the ancestral spirits. The emperors and kings who proclaimed themselves divine did not do so out of mere megalomania, but out of a real need for a unification of experience, a simplification of it, and a rooting of it in a secure source of power. The leader, like the people, senses a need for a strongly focused moral unity of the sprawling and now senseless diversity of the kingdom, and he tries to embody it in his own person:

By proclaiming themselves gods of empire, Sargon and Rameses wished to realize in their own persons that mystic or religious unity which once constituted the strength of the clan, which still maintained the unity of the kingdom, and which could alone form the tie between all the peoples of an empire. Alexander the Great, the Ptolemies, and the Caesars, will, in their turn, impose upon their subjects the worship of the sovereign, not so much out of vanity as to consolidate moral unity. . . . And so through its mystic principle the clan has survived in the empire.[9]

We see this in Hindu, Confucian, and Japanese thought as well as Near Eastern and Mediterranean thought.[10]

The New Promise of the "Era of the Son"

Christianity actually entered the confusion of the Roman world in order to simplify it and to lighten the terrible burdens of the mis-carried "sexual era," as Rank so well understood. He saw Christianity as the "era of the son" in revolt against the oppressions and inequalities of the era of the family. Under Christianity the spiritual fatherhood of Christ took the place of biological fatherhood of the family. Christ posed a totally new and radical question: "Who are my mother and my brothers?" The son was now completely independent; he could freely choose his own spiritual father and was no longer bound by the fatalities of heredity. The individual could fashion his own salvation, independent of any earthly authority. Christianity was a great democratization that put spiritual power right back into the hands of the single individual and in one blow wiped away the inequalities of the disposessed and the slaves that had gradually and inexorably developed since the breakup of the primitive world and that had assumed such grotesque proportions in the mad drivenness of the Mediterranean world. As many historical scholars have pointed out, Christianity in this sense dipped back into paganism, into primitive communalism, and extended it beyond the tribe. Rank understood this too—Christianity as a new form of democratic, universal, magical self-renewal.[11] The person recaptured some of the spiritual integrity that the primitive had enjoyed.

But as in all things human, the whole picture is ambiguous and confused, far different from the ideal promise. Actually Christianity was harnessed by the state, and its power was infused into the institution of kingship to keep its authority; the attack on the fatality of biology, the accidents of heredity, was put into the service of the ideology of the family, and it reinforced patriarchy. We still see this in Roman Catholic countries today. In other words, Christianity failed to establish the universal democratic equality that it had promised historically—the reinstitution of the sacred primitive community plus a valuation of the individual person that had not existed before. Such a revolution in thought and in social forms would have kept everything that was best in the primitive world view, and at the same time it would have liberated the person from the dead weight of communal constraint and conservatism that choked off individual initiative and development. Obviously, this failure of Christianity was intimately tied up with the general problem of class, slavery, real economic inequality. These were simply too massive and ingrained in the whole fabric of ancient society to be abolished by a new ideology. This had been the tragedy that Rome herself was unable to resolve. As Rank understood, Rome created a new type of citizen but failed to carry through and create the necessary economic equality of the families, which was the only thing that could guarantee the new structure. After all, if each man was a king in his own family, he had to be an equal king with all others; otherwise the designation lost all meaning. Theoretically, the state was dedicated to this kind of democracy because it arrogated to itself the power to hold everything in balance, to checkmate competing powers and to protect the citizens against each other. In the earlier chiefdoms, the kin groups still kept their power, and there was no one to keep them from feuding among themselves. The chief's kin group was usually the strongest, and he could punish those who attacked him, but he did not monopolize force as the later state did; he could not, for example, compel the people to go to war. The crucial characteristic of the state, and the hallmark of its genuine power and tyranny, was that it could compel its subjects to go to war. And this was because the power of each family was given over to the state; the idea was that this would prevent the social misuse of power. This made the state a kind of "power-bank," as Rank put it[12] but the state never used this power to abolish economic inequalities; as a result it actually misused the social power entrusted to it by the families and held them in unequal bondage.[13]

Christianity, too, perpetuated this economic inequality and slavishness of the would-be free, democratic citizen; *and there never has been, historically, any fundamental change in the massive structure of domination and exploitation represented by the state after the decline of primitive society.* The Reformation was a late attempt to reassert the promise of early Christianity—true individual power and equality—but it too failed by being absorbed in the unequal state scramble. It was not until World War I that the whole structure finally crumbled, after the rumbling blow given by the French Revolution: the patriarchal family, divine monarchy, the dominance of the Church, the credibility of the democratic state in its promise of true equality. The Soviets alone pushed several of these down a mine shaft along with the czar. We are struggling today in the mire of this very discredit of all overlapping traditional immortality symbols. As Rank understood, the struggle actually began at the time of the Roman Empire, and we have still not resolved it.[14] We consult astrology charts like the Babylonians, try to make our children into our own image with a firm hand like the Romans, elbow others to get a breath-quickening glimpse of the queen in her ritual procession, and confess to the priests and attend church. And we wonder why, with all this power capital drawn from so many sources, we are deeply anxious about the meaning of our lives. The reason is plain enough: none of these, nor all of them taken together, represents an integrated world conception into which we fit ourselves with pure belief and trust.

Not that the promise of the ancient world and of Christianity failed completely. Something potentially great did emerge out of them: what Rank called the "era of psychological man." We can look at it as a development out of the "era of the son." It took the form of a new kind of scientific individualism that burst out of the Renaissance and the Reformation. It represented a new power candidate for replacing all the previous ideologies of immortality, but now an almost completely and unashamedly secular one. This was a new Faustian pursuit of immortality through one's own acts, his own works, his own discovery of truth. This was a kind of secular-humanist immortality based on the gifts of the individual.

Instead of having one hero chieftain leading a tribe or a kingdom or one hero savior leading all of mankind, society would now become the breeding ground for the development of as many heroes as possible, individual geniuses in great number who would enrich mankind. This was the explicit program of Enlightenment thinkers and of the ideology of modern Jeffersonian democracy.

But alas it has been our sad experience that the new scientific Faustian man too has failed—in two resounding ways, just as Rank understood. These two ways almost all by themselves sum up the crisis of the end of our century. For one thing, modern democratic ideology simply repeated the failure of Rome and of Christianity: it did not eliminate economic inequality.[15] And so it was caught in the same fundamental and tragic contradictions as its predecessors. Second, the hope of Faustian man was that he would discover Truth, obtain the secret to the workings of nature, and so assure the complete triumph of man over nature, his apotheosis on earth. Not only has Faustian man failed to do this, but he is actually ruining the very theater of his own immortality with his own poisonous and madly driven works; once he had eclipsed the sacred dimension, he had only the earth left to testify to the value of his life. This is why, I think, even one-dimensional politicians and bureaucrats, in both capitalist and communist countries, are becoming anxious about environmental collapse; the earth is the only area of self-perpetuation in the new ideology of Faustian man.°

° Thus Rank's view of succession of "immortality-ideologies" in history. I don't want to get into a scholarly evaluation of Rank here, but only to caution the reader not to be too critical of Rank's "stages" of the evolution of consciousness. His work today gives the impression of an amateurish precision, of the kind of global judgments on history that early psychoanalysts liked to make. But this would not be fair to Rank. He was trying to put order into an immense mass of historical-psychological fact, and he forced a sharp conceptualization of it in order to "get it out" so that we could possess it and hopefully use it. I agree with Progoff's judgment that Rank was too sophisticated a scholar to hold to a rigid theory of historical stages. Cf. I. Progoff, The Death and Rebirth of Psychology (New York: Dell, 1964), pp. 209, 215. I think Rank's "eras" should be taken for the suggestive value they have, and as a basis for a really to-be-worked-out historical psychology; what they do is to bring out most forcefully the problem of immortality as a connecting thread throughout the historical forms of human arrangements. As we shall see in the next chapter, Brown brought out that other thread that cut through the "eras" and helped to blur them: the continuing immortality ideology of money.

Money: The New Universal
Immortality Ideology

The adult flight from death—the immortality
promised in all religions, the immortality of
familial corporations, the immortality of cultural
achievements—perpetuates the Oedipal project
of becoming father of oneself: adult sublimation
continues the Oedipal project. . . . Thus man
acquires a soul distinct from his body, and a
superorganic culture which perpetuates the revolt
against organic dependence on the mother. The
soul and the superorganic culture perpetuate both
the Oedipal *causa sui* project and that horror of
biological fact which is the essence of the
castration complex.
Norman O. Brown[1]

At the beginning of the last chapter I said that there were two
recent epoch-making orderings of history, and now we are ready
to take up the second—the work of Norman O. Brown. I think that
Rank and Brown taken together represent a massive double exposure of the basic motives of the human condition; I don't believe
that previous modes of thought about man in society can long
remain unaffected by their work. For his sweep over history Brown
used the identical unifying principle of Rank: the universal urge
to immortality. And so he could arrive at exactly the conclusion of
Rank: if immortality is the unchangeable motive, then all social
custom is essentially sacred.[2] One of the main contributions of
Brown's *Life against Death* was to pull together the basic ideas for
a sacred theory of money power. It is all contained in his astonish-
ing and regaling chapter titled "Filthy Lucre." As a condensed

73

synthesis of significant ideas it is one of the great essays in the history of thought. Let me just give a sketch of Brown's thesis on money, to see how it supports and confirms Rank's and how it adds its own vital insight into the evolution of new structures of power.

We saw that with the decline of the primitive world and with the rise of kingship men came to imitate kings in order to get power. Now what did kings pursue besides immortality in the royal family? Why of course: silks, courtesans, fine swords, horses and monuments, city palaces and country estates—all the things that can be bought with gold. If you gained immortality by leaving behind earthly sons, why not equally gain it by leaving behind vast accumulations of other physical mementos to your image? And so the pursuit of money was also opened up to the average man; gold became the new immortality symbol. In the temple buildings, palaces, and monuments of the new cities we see a new kind of power being generated. No longer the power of the totemic communion of persons, but the power of the testimonial of piles of stone and gold. As Brown so succinctly put it:

In monumental form, as money or as the city itself, each generation inherits the ascetic achievements of its ancestors . . . as a debt to be paid by further accumulation of monuments. Through the city the sins of the fathers are visited upon the children, every city has a history and a rate of interest.[3]

In other words, the new patriarchy passes not only family immortality to the son, but also accumulated gold, property, and interest—and the duty to accumulate these in turn. The son assures his own self-perpetuation by being "greater" than the father: by leaving behind a larger mark. Immortality comes to reside no longer in the invisible world of power, but in the very visible one, and "death is overcome by accumulating time-defying monuments. These accumulations of stone and gold make possible the discovery of the immortal soul. . . . Death is overcome on condition that the real actuality of life pass into these immortal and dead things; money is the man; the immortality of the estate or a corporation resides in the dead things which alone endure."[4] The pyramid directed its hope of immortality to the sky which it tried to penetrate, but it displayed itself before men and laid its heavy burden on their backs.

Brown gave us a more incisive picture than Rank, then, by fixing firmly on the *mechanism* of the corruption of the primitive. To carry through with our metaphor, if Rank showed the heartbeat of history, Brown exposed the material that flowed in the veins, and that material was gold. Man now took the sacred and tried to give it monumental, enduring form; it was natural, then, that in the city he finally settled upon the most durable precious metals. If the new dramatization of immortality was to be in the power and glitter of the visible rather than the invocation of the invisible, then that drama had to be transferred from the group to the new magic object, money. Money is the new "totemic" possession.[5]

This equation of money and totemic spirits is not meant to be frivolous. With the decline of tribal society, rituals were also discredited. Yet man needed new rituals because they gave order and form to society and magically tied the whole world of experience together. And this is probably the fundamental reason that money entered the picture in the ancient world with such ineluctable force: it filled the vacuum left by ritual and itself became the new ritual focus. Mary Douglas makes just this equation of money and ritual in a very powerful way:

Money provides a fixed, external, recognizable sign for what would be confused, contradictable operations; ritual makes visible external signs of internal states. Money mediates transactions; ritual mediates experience, including social experience. Money provides a standard for measuring worth; ritual standardizes situations, and so helps to evaluate them. Money makes a link between the present and the future, so does ritual. The more we reflect on the richness of the metaphor, the more it becomes clear that this is no metaphor. Money is only an extreme and specialized type of ritual.[6]

Let us see how the ritual fascination of money began in the ancient world, and how it took over as an immortality focus in itself. One of the fascinating chapters in history is the evolution of money—all the more so since it has yet to be written, as Brown says.[7] One of the reasons it isn't written is that the origin of money is shrouded in prehistory; another is that its development must have varied, must not have followed a single, universal line. Still a third reason touches closer to home: modern man seems to have trouble understanding money; it is too close to him, too much a part of his life. As someone once remarked, the last thing a fish would discover is water, since it is so unconsciously and naturally a part of its life. But beyond all this, as Brown has so well understood, the reason money is so elusive to our understanding is that it is *still sacred,* still a magical object on which we rely for our entrance into immortality. Or, put another way, money is obscure to analysis because it is still a living myth, a religion. Oscar Wilde observed that "religions die when one points out their truth. Science is the history of dead religions." From this point of view, the religion of money has resisted the revelation of its truth; it has not given itself over to science because it has not wanted to die.

How else explain that we do not yet have a sacred history of money, despite the massive collection of anthropological and historical monographs, the observations by Plato and Aristotle themselves, those by Augustine on money fetishism, the writings of Simmel and later German and French scholars, the fascinating thoughts of Spengler, the trenchant essays of A. M. Hocart, the insights of Marx, and now, finally, of modern psychoanalysis? This is where Brown's synthetic talents come into the problem: he leaned on this long tradition, including Freud's theory of anality, and raked over it all with a penetration and doggedness that reminded one of *Das Kapital.* Brown showed that despite all the expert hemmings and hawings, money was what it was—sacred power—and not another thing. There is no purpose in repeating here Brown's running argument with key authorities; let me just sum up the high points, partly from my own point of view.

We get many key insights into the early history of money, even though it is shrouded in obscurity. For one thing, anthropologists have long known that money existed on primitive levels of social life; and when we took Anthropology 1A, we were amused at the "perversity" of primitives. Imagine such bizarre things as dogs' teeth, sea shells, bands of feathers, and mats being used as money! These things not only seem to us worthless, they may even be repugnant to our sense of what is "proper" to carry around and to value. The key to the whole thing is, of course, that we live in a different power world than did the primitives. For us, motors, guns, electric circuits embody power, for the primitives, power resided in the qualities of living things and in the organs that embodied those qualities: teeth equaled biting and tearing power, with their uncanny smoothness and white luster and their terrible destructiveness to living beings; feathers equaled the freedom and miraculousness of flight; and so on.[8] These forms of primitive money, then, did not have mere ornamental value or practical exchange value as we understand it; they had real spirit-power value. And when it comes to the evolution of our own money we must look to the same source, to its origin in magic amulets or tokens, as Brown—basing himself on Laum—understood.

The noted historian G. Eliot Smith put together an interesting speculation on the origin of gold as a thing of great value in ancient Egypt. What leads man to assign great value to something? That it gives life, enables man to triumph over weakness and death by borrowing some of the powers of the gods. Eliot Smith put together the following development: There was a cowrie shell in the Red Sea which came to be prized as a token of life-giving powers, as an amulet to ward off the danger of death and to prolong the existence of the souls of those already dead. It was an immortality symbol, then, that came to be identified with the goddess Hathor, the divine cow, the Great Mother. Eliot Smith says:

The people of Egypt began to make models of these and other magical shells in clay, stone and any other material that came to hand. These were believed to have the magic of the real shells. . . . In the course [of time they] discovered that they could make durable and attractive models by using the soft plastic metal which was lying around unused and unappreciated in the Nubian desert. . . . The lightness and beauty of the untarnishable yellow metal made an instant appeal. The gold models soon became more popular than the original shells, and the reputation for life-giving was then in large measure transferred from the mere form of the amulet to the metal itself.[9]

In other words, the powers of the god came to be present in the metal.

In India, as Hocart so clearly showed, gold was straightforwardly identified with the fire god Agni. Gold could be substituted for

the sun in the sacred ritual. Hocart quotes this telling passage from
the *Satapatha Brahamana:*

For this gold plate is the same as truth. Yonder sun is the same as
truth. It is made of gold: for gold is light, and he (the sun) is light;
gold is immortality, and he is immortality; it is round, for he is round. . . .
Indeed, this gold plate is the sun.[10]

Hocart, in his masterful little essay, "Money," suggests a common
origin for the gold coin, the crown, and the halo, since all three
represent the sun's disc. (We liked to imagine that we knew coins
were round because they could fit more comfortably in our pock-
ets.) The great economist Keynes agreed that the special attraction
of gold and silver as primary monetary values was due to their
symbolic identification with the sun and the moon, which occupied
a primary sacred place in the early "cosmic government" cosmolo-
gies. Even more fascinating is the fact that the value ratio of gold
and silver has remained stable from classical antiquity through the
Middle Ages and even into modern times as 1:13½. Brown agrees
with Laum that such a stability cannot be explained in logical terms
of rational supply and demand: the explanation must lie in the
astrological ratio of the cycles of the divine counterparts of these
metals—the sun and moon.[11] We have forgotten how tenacious
astrological magic has been in history, even in the face of its vitality
still today. Man has always sought to discover the special magical
properties in nature and to bring them to bear in his life. The
ancients sought these special qualities in qualities of living things,
in natural miraculous objects like the sun, and in the ratios they
could tease out of nature. Until very modern times, to take one
example, musical instruments were built in magical astrological
proportions so as to make the most divinely harmonious sounds;
and I personally know one inspired guitar maker who uses the
ancient "Greek foot" as a basic measure.

Currency, then, seems to have had its origin in magic amulets
and magic imitations of the sun, which were worn or stored because they contained the protecting spirit powers. If gold had any
"utility," as Hocart says, it was a supernatural utility: "a little of
it was given away in exchange for quantities of stuff because a few

ounces of divinity were worth pounds of gross matter."[12] And so we see how it was that money came to buy many other things: if it was magic, people would give anything to have it. As Géza Róheim put it in a very happy formulation, "originally people do not desire money because you can buy things for it, but you can buy things for money because people desire it.[13]

If gold was sacred, we can now understand—with Simmel and Hocart—how it was that the first banks were temples and the first ones to issue money were the priests. With the ascendancy of priestcraft it became the priests themselves who monopolized the official traffic in sacred charms and in the exchange of favors for gold. The first mints were set up in the temples of the gods, whence our word "money"—from the mint in the temple of Juno Moneta, Juno the admonisher, on the Capitoline Hill in Rome. Forgery was sacrilege because the coins embodied the powers of the gods and only the priests could handle such powers; we get the same feeling about counterfeiters today, that they are practicing an unspeakable usurpation of hallowed powers.

The temples, then, were clearinghouses for money transactions, just like banks today. It was surely not lost on the priests—the first leisure class—that the tiniest quantity of sacred gold-power could bring in huge amounts of food and other stuffs. Priests may have talents for dealing with the supernatural, but they have very human appetite (and often lots of it); and if they have the leisure to ply their trade, it is because since earliest times they have convinced their fellows that it is important to assure that leisure by bringing part of the fruit of the sweat of their brow to the priests. And so the food producers must have brought food to the temples in exchange for prayers and sacrifices being performed on their behalf. Also, it must have worked the other way too: gold was a fee paid to the priest for his intercessions with the invisible powers. As Hocart pointed out, in India the gold fee was the proper one to pay to a god, whose essence was gold.[14] Whence the tradition of the earliest coins being imprinted with the images of gods, then divine kings, down to presidents in our time. All visitors to the most holy temples could bring back with them gold encapsulations of sacred power that would keep them safe throughout the year. As we finger, in our pocket, the face on the silver dollar, we re-experience some of the quiet confidence of the ancients who left the temples with their life-securing charms. Today clerics similarly finger the souvenir medallions of their visit to holy Rome, and over the years they wear away the face of the Pope on these medallions. The Pope's power is present in the effigy just like the god's was in the coin.

We know that the priests were part of the immortality ideology of what has aptly been called "cosmic government" and "the astro-biological unification of divine kingship." We have already described the hierarchy: the king got his powers from the heavens and radiated them in his own person to the people with the help of the priests, to the benefit of the patriarchal families. We might say that money coinage fit beautifully into this scheme, because now the cosmic powers could be the property of everyman, without even the need to visit temples: you could now traffic in immortality in the marketplace. Nor is this just a manner of speaking, for this traffic was a most serious new business that arose. Admittedly, when we reconstruct the phenomenological history of money it is impossible for us moderns to "get into the mind and behind the eyes" of the ancient negotiators. But a new man emerged in the ancient world, a man who based the value of his life—and so of his immortality—on a new cosmology centered on coins. We can't very well grasp what the painting visible even today at the entrance of a house in the ruins of Pompeii meant to the owner of the house or to the passerby whom it was obviously supposed to impress. But a picture of a man proudly weighing his penis in a scale of gold coins must convey a feeling that the powers of nature as exemplified in the reproductive life force have their equivalency in gold, even perhaps that fatherhood is given by gold as well as the penis—and generally that the *causa sui* project is well in hand. And the two chests of coins just inside the entrance, adjacent to the sleeping rooms of the adult occupants, surely convey the new way of life based on the feeling in the painting. Money became the distilled value of all existence, as Spengler seems to have understood so well:

When . . . Corinth was destroyed, the melting-down of the statues for coinage and the auctioning of the inhabitants at the slave-mart were, for Classical minds, one and the same operation—the transformation of corporeal objects into money.[15]

Or, we might say, into a single immortality symbol, *a ready way of relating the increase of oneself* to all the important objects and events of one's world. In this sense, money seems to have represented a cosmological unification of visible and invisible powers—powers of the gods, of kings, of heroic victors in war—and the distillation of the booty of war. And at the center of this cosmology stood the person himself with the visible counters of his own increase, the divine testimonial to his own immortal worth, distilling and spanning both worlds.

It is along lines such as these that we have to understand the meaning of money, from its very inception in prehistory and from its explosive development with the invention of coinage in the ancient world. Money is sacred as all cultural things are sacred. As Rank taught us and as Brown so powerfully reaffirmed, "Custom is . . . essentially sacred"—and why should money be any exception?[16] The thing that connects money with the domain of the sacred is its *power*. We have long known that money gives power over men, freedom from family and social obligations, from friends, bosses, and underlings; it abolishes one's likeness to others; it creates comfortable distance between persons, easily satisfies their claims on each other without compromising them in any direct and personal way; on top of this it gives literally limitless ability to satisfy appetites of almost any material kind. Power is not an economic category, and neither is it simply a social category: "All power is essentially sacred power."[17] This is perfect. All power is in essence power to deny mortality. Either that or it is not real power at all, not ultimate power, not the power that mankind is really obsessed with. Power means power to increase oneself, to change one's natural situation from one of smallness, helplessness, finitude, to one of bigness, control, durability, importance. In its power to manipulate physical and social reality money in some ways secures one against contingency and accident; it buys bodyguards, bullet-proof glass, and better medical care. Most of all, it can be accumulated and passed on, and so radiates its powers even after one's death, giving one a semblance of immortality as he lives in the vicarious enjoyments of his heirs that his money continues to buy, or in the magnificence of the art works that he commissioned, or in the statues of himself and the majesty of his own mausoleum. In short, money is the human mode *par excellence* of coolly denying animal boundness, the determinism of nature.

And here Brown takes issue with orthodox Freudian theory and makes a real improvement on it, makes it amenable to our understanding in one of its most inverted and esoteric areas. We have always been put off when psychoanalysts equated money with feces—it seemed so crass and unreal. We cannot imagine pure pleasure in playing with feces; even to children feces are ambivalent and to some degree distasteful. If as tiny infants they play with feces, it is at a time when feces can have no precise meaning to them; if later on they play with feces, this is already a different kind of play, a play of mastery of anxiety, a dealing with a very ambivalent area of experience. Also, it has always seemed simplistic to say that money equals feces, because money has been so supercharged with the yearning of ambition and hope; it could not be merely infantile smearing, not simple self-indulgence. In fact, as Brown has so well argued, money does not equal feces at all, does not represent them at all: rather, it represents the *denial* of feces, of physicalness, of animality, of decay and death.

To rise above the body is to equate the body with excrement. In the last analysis, the peculiar human fascination with excrement is the peculiar human fascination with death.[18]

Money is associated with the anal region because it represents *par excellence* the abstract cultural mode of linking man with transcendent powers. As Marx so unfailingly understood, it is the perfect "fetish" for an ape-like animal who bemuses himself with striking icons. Money sums up the *causa sui* project all in itself: how man, with the tremendous ingenuity of his mind and the materials of his earth, can contrive the dazzling glitter, the magical ratios, the purchase of other men and their labors, to link his destiny with the stars and live down his animal body.[19] The only hint we get of the cultural repression seeping through is that even dedicated financiers wash their hands after handling money. The victory over death is a fantasy that cannot be fully believed in; money doesn't entirely banish feces, and so the threat of germs and vulnerability in the very process of securing immortality. If we say that "money is God," this seems like a simple and cynical observation on the corruptibility of men. But if we say that "money negotiates immortality and therefore is God," this is a scientific formula that is limpidly objective to any serious student of man.

Nor do we have to dig back into prehistory and conjecture on what money meant to the ancient Greeks or Pompeiians. We see the change from tribal modes of achieving power to money modes right before our eyes: the drama of early Athenian society is repeated in any area where detribalization is taking place. Tempels's comment on the modern Bantu eloquently sums up the new man who emerged in history and continues to emerge:

Recently I have heard Bantu of the old school say, with reference to our modern product, the Europeanized *évolués* "These are men of *lupeto* (money)." They have explained to me that these Europeanized young men of ours know nothing but money, that it is the only thing possessing any value for them. They . . . give up their Bantu philosophy . . . for a philosophy of money. Money is their one and only ideal, their end and the supreme ultimate norm regulating their actions. . . . Everything . . . has been destroyed by this new value, this modern universal rule of conduct: *lupeto*, money.[20]

How to understand this obsessive, fanatical shift that occurs in one generation, right under the eyes of the elders, except to see it as a hunger for self-perpetuation, a hunger driven by the discredit into which the traditional immortality ideology has fallen? The rapid and utter disintegration of tribal society has always been, historically, the result of the discredit of old sources of immortalizing powers and the belief that the new ways of life brought by the foreigners contain the genuine, the stronger powers. The old group no longer gives life, and so the young chuck the social obligations in favor of real, new power over men and things. Missionary activity has gone hand in hand with superior weapons and medicines because the priests have always known that they have to prove that their god represents superior powers. Think; if a race of men with advanced learning, health, and weapons were to land on our planet and tell us about the god who sustains them in Alpha Centauri, a new religion would sweep over large numbers of people overnight and discredit most of our institutions.

Thus money has been the single red line connecting the various failed historical ideologies of immortality—from *lupeto* men called by a hundred other tribal names, through Pompeii, through the buying of indulgences in the Middle Ages, through Calvin and modern commercialism. Underneath the different historical forms of immortality striving has pulsated the lifeblood of money. In this sense, the social-structural forms of immortality striving that succeeded each other up to modern times have been a kind of mask or façade over the deeper-going immortality symbol, money. Rank didn't talk about this dualism, but he surely understood it. He spoke about the failure of the ideology of democracy to really do what it promised—to make everyone economically and socially equal. Remember we saw that Roman patriarchy failed to do this, as did Christianity. How explain this failure of an immortality ideology to give what it promises, except to say that at some deeper level it is all the while giving *another kind* of immortality? Otherwise men would not have it at all. As Rank put it, in a phrase that he left enigmatic, economic equality is "beyond the endurance of the democratic type" of man.[21] How to understand such an unsettling and radical idea, except by a psychology of money as sacred power? Money gives power *now*—and, through accumulated property, land, and interest, power in the future. Man has become dependent on social symbols of prestige that single him out as especially worthy of being remembered in the eyes of the gods and in the minds of men. But for an animal who actually lives on the level of the visible and knows nothing of the invisible, it is easy for the eyes of men to take precedence over the eyes of the gods. The symbols of immortal power that money buys exist on the level of the visible, and so crowd out their invisible competitor. Man succumbs easily to the temptation of created life, which is to exercise power mainly in the dimension in which he moves and acts as an organism. The pull of the body is so strong, lived experience is so direct; the "supernatural" is so remote and problematic, so abstract and intangible. This is what Buñuel wanted to show with his feasting and corrupt priests in the film *Tristana:* even the ones who claim to give priority to the invisible cannot fight the pull of appetite for wine and meat, the prerogatives and security that money gives. And this, too, of course, is the traditional meaning of the symbol of the Devil: he represents physical, earthly, visible power and on this planet easily holds sway over his more ethereal competitor, spiritual power. This is what theologians have meant when they have said that on this earth God must obey the Devil.[22] The earth runs on physical laws. The Devil, in Buñuel's film, is the human head striking inside the church bell, the living flesh that hopelessly corrupts the ethereal music.

No wonder economic equality is beyond the endurance of modern democratic man: the house, the car, the bank balance are his immortality symbols. Or, put another way, if a black man moves next door, it is not merely that your house diminishes in real estate value, but that *you* diminish in fullness on the level of visible immortality and so you *die. Things* have given immortality probably since the rise of the earliest states, but in modern times this one-dimensionality of the level of the visible has run wild. For one thing, the decline of traditional religion has eclipsed the god whose eyes judged merit according to the goods you piled up. Hand in hand with this, the ideology of modern commercialism has unleashed a life of invidious comparison unprecedented in history, as Scheler and others understood. In other words, modern man cannot endure economic equality because he has no faith in self-transcendent, otherworldly immortality symbols; visible physical worth is the only thing he has to give him eternal life.[23] No wonder that people segregate themselves with such consuming dedication, that specialness is so much a fight to the death: man lashes out all the harder when he is cornered, when he is a pathetically impoverished immortality seeker. He dies when his little symbols of specialness die. Occasionally modern man is moved to philosophize on the human condition, and stumbles on the great insight that "you can't take it with you." This leads him to pause and heave a sigh over the perversity of nature, but it doesn't really touch him, since he leaves behind precisely the immortal marks of his own achievement.* He might feel self-pity and bitterness about the one-dimensionality of his immortality, but in matters of eternity you take what you can get.

No wonder, either, that the other modern ideology of egalitarianism has also found real economic equality to be unendurable. Are we puzzled that the Soviets create new prestige classes, push the patriarchal family and the careers of their children, and pursue money and goods? They too exist only on the level of the visible, and must somehow secure their immortality here. At the beginning of the revolution they got immortality by merging with the "totemic" group soul of revolutionary activity; now they must try to establish the marks of each one's personal merit. This is one of the reasons, finally, that primitive Christianity is a real threat to both commercialism and communism, at least when it takes its own message seriously. Primitive Christianity is one of the few ideologies that has kept alive the idea of the invisible dimension of nature and the priority of this dimension for assuring immortality. Thus it is a threat to any one-dimensional immortality ideology, and could work in a democracy that modern democratic man himself finds too burdensome, a society free of class and race struggle, because symbols of class and race prestige don't carry weight in the realm of the invisible spirit. The Pope's recent declaration celebrating the eightieth anniversary of the first social-problem encyclical is an eloquent reminder of how early Christian radicalism rumbles under the one-dimensional obsessiveness of modern industrial life. Christianity is still an almost pure "primitive" accusation of the corruptions of *lupeto*, of 2,500 years of history.

---

* I think it is along these lines, too, that the assertion that primitive societies were often paranoid makes sense. Anyone who distinguished himself by too many exploits accrued too much power, and so he was a danger to the group. Since primitives did not have the legal apparatus for protecting the group against strong individuals, they were naturally feared; and so there was a sort of built-in pressure for keeping things level and power in balance. Cf. Franz Borkenau's comment in his rich essay "The Concept of Death," *The Twentieth Century*, 1955, 157:317.

The Demonics of History

Immortality power, then, came to reside in accumulated wealth. And once individuals and families were free to negotiate their value in this kind of coinage, there was no stopping the process. One of the merits of Brown's analysis is that he saw, with Eliade, how necessary to this new development was the change in notions of time. Primitive man lived in a world devoid of clocks, progressive calendars, once only numbered years. Nature was seen in her imagined purity of endless cycles of sun risings and settings, moon waxings and wanings, seasons changing, animals dying and being born, etc. This kind of cosmology is not favorable to the accumulation of either guilt or property, since everything is wiped away with the gifts and nature is renewed with the help of ritual ceremonies of regeneration. Man did not feel that he had to pile things up. Brown makes the excellent point that it is not quite true to say that primitive man lived in an "eternal now": he experienced the flow of time because he experienced guilt. That is, in terms of our discussion of guilt, primitive man lived in certain universal binds that characterize human life, and so he had to experience time flow because these binds are composed with the passage of time. Guilt and time, then, are inseparable, which is why primitive man so elaborately tried to deny them both with regenerative rituals.[24] It took the longest time for this denial to be given up; the Greeks and Romans were reluctant to admit that the old regenerative rituals no longer worked. Probably the repeated sackings of Rome graphically swung the balance. It could no longer be pretended that the ancient rituals of renewal could keep regenerating the city, and at this time growing numbers of people opted for Christianity, which promised the impending end of the world; after Augustine, time was firmly set in a linear way while waiting for that end. We are still today ticking off the years, but we no longer know what for, unless it is for compounding interest, as Brown argues. Compounding interest is one of the few meaningful things to do in an irreversible time stream that is wholly secular and visible.

No wonder the confusion of the ancient world was so great and tension and anxiety were so high: men had already amassed great burdens of guilt by amassing possessions, and there was no easy way to atone for this. Men were no longer safely tucked into the group, but they still had their human burdens. As Brown puts it, men were still in flight from themselves, from their own mortality.[25] The burden of time, the tension between the visible and the invisible worlds, and the guilt of possessions must have been high on sensitive souls. This is how we understand the growth of the notion of "sin" historically. Theologically, sin means literally separation from the powers and protection of the gods, a setting up of oneself as a *causa sui*. Sin is the experience of uncertainty in one's relation to the divine ground of his being; he no longer is sure of possessing the right connection, the right means of expiation. He feels alone, exposed, weighed down by the burden of guilt accumulated in this world by the acts of his body and his material desires. His experience of the *physicalness* of life obsesses him. Modern missionaries found that the notion of sin was difficult to translate to primitives, who had no word for it; we understand now that they had little experience of isolation or separateness from the group or the ancestral pool of souls.[26] The experience of sin still today, for simple believers, is merely one of "uncleanliness" and straightforward prohibition of specific acts. It is not the experience of one's whole life as a problem.

No wonder that early converts to Christianity could renounce everything in a decisive way that today seems strangely self-sacrificial to us. We are not in the same bind. We have completely eclipsed the tension of the invisible-visible dichotomy by simply denying the invisible world. We have put time on a wholly unilinear basis, and so money and cumulative interest have become our unequivocal god. Christianity proved to be an idealistic interlude that failed; and so we have reaffirmed the ancient pursuit of wealth with a vengeance and straightforward dedication of which archaic man was incapable. We have become completely secular. Accordingly, we no longer have any problem with sin, since there is nothing to be separated from: everything is *here*, in one's possessions, in his body. There is no experience of sin where the body is not felt to be a problem, where one imagines that he does indeed have full control over his own destiny on the *physical level alone.* Separation from the divine powers is not felt because these powers are *denied* by the primary power of the visible things. In other words, we have succeeded better than even the primitives in avoiding sin, by simply denying the existence of the invisible dimension to which it is related. In contrast with guilt, we don't even have to repress it, since it does not arise in our experience of the world.

Brown points out that the secularization of the economy means that we can no longer be redeemed by work, since the creation of a surplus is no longer addressed as a gift to the gods. Which means that the new god Money that we pursue so dedicatedly is not a god that gives expiation! It is perverse. We wonder how we could allow ourselves to do *this* to ourselves, but right away we know the answer: we didn't take command of history at some given point where civilization started. Not even the noble and thoughtful Athenians could manage that. Rather, history took command of us in our original drivenness toward heroism; and our urge to heroism has always taken the nearest means at hand. Brown says that the result of this secularization process is that we have an economy "driven by the pure sense of guilt, unmitigated by any sense of redemption."[27] What has happened to guilt? It is "repressed by denial into the unconscious"—which can only mean that we are "more uncontrollably driven" by it. Another way of putting this is to say that man has changed from the giving animal, the one who passes things on, to the wholly taking and keeping one. By continually taking and piling and computing interest and leaving to one's heirs, man contrives the illusion that he is in complete control of his destiny. After all, accumulated things are a visible testimonial to power, to the fact that one is not limited or dependent. Man imagines that the *causa sui* project is firmly in his hands, that he is the heroic maker and doer who takes what he creates, what is rightfully his. And so we see how modern man, in his one-dimensional economics, is driven by the lie of his life, by his denial of limitation, of the true state of natural affairs.

If we sum it all up historically, we seem to be able to say that man became a greater victim of his drivenness when heroism pushed expiation out of the picture; man was now giving expression to only one side of his nature. He still needs expiation for the peace of his life because he is stuck with his natural and universal experience of guilt. Brown says that the "man who takes is strong enough to shoulder his own guilt," that the process of expiation of modern man "has been reified and passes into piles of stone and gold."[28] Granted that money represents the new *causa sui* project, that the infantile omnipotence is no longer in one's body but in things. But to repress guilt is not to "shoulder" it; it is not that guilt has vanished by being transmuted into things or expiated by things; rather, as Freud taught us, that which is denied must come out by some other means. History is the tragic record of heroism and expiation out of control and of man's efforts to earn expiation in new, frantically driven and contrived ways. The burden of guilt created by cumulative possessions, linear time, and secularization is assuredly greater than that experienced by primitive man; it has to come out some way.

The point I am making is that most of the evil that man has visited on his world is the result precisely of the greater passion of his denials and his historical drivenness. This leads us directly from problems of psychoanalysis and history right up to the problem of the science of man itself: what is the nature of evil in human affairs, and how can we come to grips with it as thoughtful men trying to take back some control over our own destiny, trying to fish ourselves out of the whirlpool of our historical passion? The only way that seems open to reason is to continue to try to soberly sort out our own motives, those that have led to our present state.

CHAPTER SEVEN

The Basic Dynamic of Human Evil

> All our human problems, with their intolerable
> sufferings, arise from man's ceaseless attempts to
> make this material world into a man-made reality
> . . . aiming to achieve on earth a "perfection"
> which is only to be found in the beyond . . .
> thereby hopelessly confusing the values of both
> spheres.
> Otto Rank[1]

These words by Otto Rank, if read quickly, seem like a wise enough commentary on human folly: we always knew man tried to achieve the impossible, that he was a proud, confused, and stubborn animal and that because of it he got into mischief. Like a puppy with a shoe or a kitten with a ball of string, man tends to endear himself to us because of the swashbuckling ways in which he tries to grasp reality. But Rank's words are not a mere commentary about an endearing, pathetic, and confused animal. They are much more than that: they are a complete scientific formula about the cause of evil in human affairs. We know today that the world-historical importance of psychoanalysis is precisely that it has revealed to us the dynamics of human misery.

You can see this most clearly not in the works of Freud, but in those who dissented from his work. Take three disparate thinkers like Otto Rank, Wilhelm Reich, and Carl Jung. There is nothing to identify them with one another except that they dissented from Freud; each had his own work and distinctive style, sometimes at a polar opposite from the other dissenters. What two people are more dissimilar than Reich and Jung? Yet at the bottom of all this unlikeness there is the fact of a fundamental agreement on what exactly causes evil in human affairs. This is not a remarkable coincidence: it is a solid scientific achievement that argues for the basic truth of what the dissenters found.

We have already had a preview of this truth in our overview of history with Rank: that man wants above all to endure and prosper, to achieve immortality in some way. Because he knows he is mortal, the thing he wants most to deny is this mortality. Mortality is connected to the natural, animal side of his existence; and so man reaches beyond and away from that side. So much so that he tries to deny it completely. As soon as man reached new historical forms of power, he turned against the animals with whom he had previously identified—with a vengeance, we now see, because the animals embodied what man feared most, a nameless and faceless death.

I have shown elsewhere that the whole edifice of Rank's superb thought is built on a single foundation stone: man's fear of life and death. There is no point repeating this here except to remind us why these fundamental motives are so well hidden from ourselves. After all, it took the genius of Freud and the whole psychoanalytic movement to uncover and document the twin fears of life and death. The answer is that men do not actually live stretched openly on a rack of cowardice and terror; if they did, they couldn't continue on with such apparent equanimity and thoughtlessness. Men's fears are buried deeply by repression, which gives to everyday life its tranquil façade; only occasionally does the desperation show through, and only for some people. It is repression, then, that great discovery of psychoanalysis, that explains how well men can hide their basic motivations even from themselves. But men also live in a dimension of carefreeness, trust, hope, and joy which gives them a buoyancy beyond that which repression alone could give. This, as we saw with Rank, is achieved by the symbolic engineering of culture, which everywhere serves men as an antidote to terror by giving them a new and durable life beyond that of the body.

At about the same time that Rank wrote, Wilhelm Reich also based his entire work on the same few basic propositions. In a few wonderful pages in *The Mass Psychology of Fascism* Reich lays bare the dynamic of human misery on this planet: it all stems from man trying to be other than he is, trying to deny his animal nature. This, says Reich, is the cause of all psychic illness, sadism, and war. The guiding principles of the formation of all human ideology "harp on the same monotonous tune: 'We are not animals. . . .' "[2]

In his book Reich is out to explain fascism, why men so willingly give over their destiny to the state and the great leader. And he explains it in the most direct way: it is the politician who promises to engineer the world, to raise man above his natural destiny, and so men put their whole trust in him. We saw how easily men passed from egalitarian into kingship society, and for that very reason: because the central power promised to give them unlimited immunities and prosperities. We will see in the next chapter how this new arrangement unleashed on mankind regular and massive miseries that primitive societies encountered only occasionally and usually on a small scale. Men tried to avoid the natural plagues of existence by giving themselves over to structures which embodied immunity power, but they only succeeded in laying waste to themselves with the new plagues unleashed by their obedience to the politicians. Reich coined the apt term "political plague mongers" to describe all politicians. They are the ones who lied to people about the real and the possible and launched mankind on impossible dreams which took impossible tolls of real life. Once you base your whole life-striving on a desperate lie and try to implement that lie, try to make the world just the opposite of what it is, then you instrument your own undoing. The theory of the German superman—or any other theory of group or racial superiority—"has its origin in man's effort to disassociate himself from the animal." All you have to do is to say that your group is pure and good, eligible for a full life and for some kind of eternal meaning. But others like Jews or Gypsies are the real animals, are spoiling everything for you, contaminating your purity and bringing disease and weakness into your vitality. Then you have a mandate to launch a political plague, a campaign to make the world pure. It is all in Hitler's *Mein Kampf*, in those frightening pages about how the Jews lie in wait in the dark alleys ready to infect young German virgins with syphilis. Nothing more theoretically basic needs to be said about the general theory of scapegoating in society—although we will look at it in more detail in the next chapter.

Reich asks why hardly anyone knows the names of the real benefactors of mankind, whereas "every child knows the name of the generals of the political plague?" The answer is that:

Natural science is constantly drilling into man's consciousness that fundamentally he is a worm in the universe. The political plague-monger is constantly harping upon the fact that man is not an animal, but a "zoon politikon," i.e., a non-animal, an upholder of values, a "moral being." How much mischief has been perpetuated by the Platonic philosophy of the state! It is quite clear why man knows the politicos better than the natural scientists: He does not want to be reminded of the fact that he is fundamentally a sexual animal. *He does not want to be an animal.*[3]

I give Reich's view of the dynamic of evil without any technical adornment because I don't think that it needs any. But there is plenty of adornment in the psychoanalytic literature, for anyone who wants to follow out the intricate theoretical workings of the psyche. The marvelous thing about psychoanalytic theory is that it took simple statements about the human condition, such as man's denial of his own animality, and showed how this denial was grounded in the psyche from earliest childhood. Thus psychoanalysts talk about "good" objects and "bad" ones, about "paranoid" stages of development, "denials," "split-off" segments of the psyche which includes a "death enclave," etc.

In my view no one has summed up these complex psychic workings better than Jung did in his own poetic scientific way by talking about the "shadow" in each human psyche. To speak of the shadow is another way of referring to the individual's sense of creature inferiority, the thing he wants most to deny. As Erich Neumann so succinctly summed up the Jungian view:

The shadow is the other side. It is the expression of our own imperfection and earthliness, the negative which is incompatible with the absolute values [i.e., the horror of passing life and the knowledge of death].[4]

As Jung put it, the shadow becomes a dark thing in one's own psyche, "an inferiority which none the less really exists even though only dimly suspected."[5] The person wants to get away from this inferiority, naturally; he wants to "jump over his own shadow." The most direct way of doing this is by "looking for everything dark, inferior, and culpable in *others*."[6]

Men are not comfortable with guilt, it chokes them, literally is the shadow that falls over their existence. Neumann sums it up again very nicely:

> The guilt-feeling is attributable . . . to the apperception of the shadow. . . . This guilt-feeling based on the existence of the shadow is discharged from the system in the same way both by the individual and the collective—that is to say, by the phenomenon of the *projection of the shadow*. The shadow, which is in conflict with the acknowledged values [i.e., the cultural façade over animality] cannot be accepted as a negative part of one's own psyche and is therefore projected—that is, it is transferred to the outside world and experienced as an outside object. It is combated, punished, and exterminated as "the alien out there" instead of being dealt with as one's own inner problem.[7]

And so, as Neumann concludes, we have the dynamics for the classic and age-old expedient for discharging the negative forces of the psyche and the guilt: scapegoating. It is precisely the split-off sense of inferiority and animality which is projected onto the scapegoat and then destroyed symbolically with him. When all explanations are compared on the slaughter of the Jews, Gypsies, Poles, and so many others by the Nazis, and all the many reasons are adduced, there is one reason that goes right into the heart and mind of each person, and that is the projection of the shadow. No wonder Jung could observe—even more damningly than Rank or Reich—that "the principal and indeed the only thing that is wrong with the world is man."[8]

Let us now look at how this dynamic functioned in other historical contexts and at some of the other things that feed into it.

CHAPTER EIGHT

The Nature of Social Evil

Nor can we deny that we all eat and that each
of us has grown strong on the bodies of innumer-
able animals. Here each of us is a king in a field
of corpses.
Elias Canetti[1]

We have seen with Rank that the driving force behind evil in
human affairs stems from man's paradoxical nature: in the flesh and
doomed with it, out of the flesh in the world of symbols and trying
to continue on a heavenly flight. The thing that makes man the
most devastating animal that ever stuck his neck up into the sky
is that he wants a stature and a destiny that is impossible for an
animal; he wants an earth that is not an earth but a heaven, and
the price for this kind of fantastic ambition is to make the earth
an even more eager graveyard than it naturally is.

Our great wistfulness about the world of primitive man is that
he managed willy-nilly to blunt the terrible potential destructiveness of the drama of heroism and expiation. He didn't have the
size, the technological means, or the world view for running amok
heroically. Heroism was small scale and more easily controlled:
each person, as a contributor to the generative ritual, could be a
true cosmic hero who added to the powers of creation. Allied to
this cosmic heroism was a kind of warfare that has always made
military men chuckle. Among the Plains Indians it was a kind of
athletic contest in which one scored points by touching the enemy;
often it was a kind of disorganized, childish, almost hysterical game
in which one went into rapture if he brought back a trophy or a
single enemy for torture. Anyone was liable to be snatched out of
his hut at daybreak, and on mountainous islands like those of
Polynesia groups lived in continual fear of those just over the

ridge or across the lagoon; no one was ever safe from capture and sacrificial slaughter. This is hardly the ideal of altruism, and there are very few today who have a romantic image of primitive man's peaceful nature; one look at the blunt stone sacrificial slave-killing knives of the Northwest Coast Indians is enough to set the record straight. Since we do not experience the terror of the occasional victims of primitive raids, we can look back nostalgically at the small numbers consumed at random, and compare them with those who died in one day at Dresden or one flash at Hiroshima.

Rousseau had already wistfully observed the comparatively low toll of life that primitive warfare took,[2] and a whole tradition of social analysts including Marx agreed with him. Recently, when Lewis Mumford put the crown on a lifetime of brilliant work, he reaffirmed this perspective on history.[3] Today we are agreed that the picture looks something like this: that once mankind got the means for large-scale manipulation of the world, the lust for power began to take devastating tolls. This can be seen strikingly at the rise of the great civilizations based on divine kingship. These new states were structures of domination which absorbed the tribal life around them and built up empires. Masses of men were forged into obedient tools for really large-scale power operations directed by a powerful, exploitative class. It was at this time that slaves were firmly compartmentalized into various special skills which they plied monotonously; they became automaton objects of the tyrannical rulers. We still see this degradation of tribal peoples today, when they hire themselves out for money to work monotonously in the mines. Primitive man could be transformed, in one small step, from a rich creator of meaning in a society of equals to a mechanical thing.

Something was accomplished by this new organization of labor that primitive man never dreamed of, a tremendous increase in the size of human operations: huge walled cities, colossal monuments, pyramids, irrigation projects, unprecedented wars of booty and plunder. Mumford's contribution of insight into all this was to call it a "megamachine." The amalgam of kingship with sacred power, human sacrifice, and military organization unleashed a nightmare megamachine on the world—a nightmare, says Mumford, that began at Sumer and that still haunts us today, with our recent history of megamachines in Warsaw, Hiroshima, and Vietnam. This is the colossus of power gone mad, a colossus based on the dehumanization of man that began, not with Newtonian materialism, Enlightenment rationalism, or nineteenth-century commercialism, but with the first massive exploitation of men in the great divine kingships of the ancient world. It was then that man was thrown out of the mutualities of tribalism into the cauldron of historic alienation. We are still stewing there today because we have not seen that the worship of the demonic megamachine has been our fate, and we have willingly perpetuated it and even aggravated it until it threatens to destroy the very world.

From the point of view of a Marxist level of analysis, this perspective on history attacks social evil at its most obvious point. From the very beginning the ravages of large-scale warfare were partly a function of the new structure of domination called the state; the state was an instrument of oppression that had come into being "artificially" through conquest, and with it began mankind's real woes. The new class society of conquerors and slaves right away had its own internal frictions; what better way to siphon them off than by directing the energies of the masses outward toward an "alien" enemy? The state had its own built-in wisdom; it "solved" its ponderous *internal* problems of social justice by making justice a matter of triumph over an *external* enemy. This was the start of the large-scale scapegoating that has consumed such mountains of lives down through history and continues to do so today, right up to Vietnam and Bangladesh: what better way to forge a nation into a unity, to take everyone's eyes off the frightening state of domestic affairs, than by focusing on a heroic foreign cause? Mumford very pointedly summed up the psychology of this new scapegoating of the state:

Hence the sense of joyful release that so often has accompanied the outbreak of war . . . popular hatred for the ruling classes was cleverly diverted into a happy occasion to mutilate or kill *foreign* enemies.

In short, the oppressor and the oppressed, instead of fighting it out within the [ancient] city, directed their aggression toward a common goal —an attack on a rival city. Thus the greater the tensions and the harsher the daily repressions of civilization, the more useful war became as a safety valve."[4]

The Marxist argument discussed above—and it is now an agreed one—is that the new structure of the conquest state forced an increased butchery of war. Mumford very aptly reasoned that in this sense "the invention of the military machine made war 'necessary' and even desirable." With the advent of the megamachines, power simply got out of hand—or rather, got pressed into the service of a few hands—and instead of isolated and random sacrifices on behalf of a fearful tribe, ever larger numbers of people were deliberately and methodically drawn into a "dreadful ceremony" on behalf of the few. So that the "ability to wage war and to impose collective human sacrifice has remained the identifying mark of all sovereign power throughout history."[5] Little does it matter that modern public relations and the appearance of bureaucratic neutrality and efficiency disguise better than ever both the sacrifice and the blatant central power of the state; the chief of the U.S. "Selective Service" (the public relations euphemism) may sit around and logically explain his function and the "fairness" of the selective process to young high school students, but the bare fact is that they are obliged by the state's power to offer their lives for its own diversionary ceremony, just as were the ancient Egyptian slaves. If there is anything new in all this, it is that the young are beginning to understand what is really happening.

Why has mankind remained locked into such a demonism of power all through history? It is not simply because the slaves have not had the power to throw off their chains; or, as the early Marxists argued, simply because men have forgotten how it was "in the beginning" before the state stepped on their necks. Mumford goes beyond this into a psychological level of analysis and answers that the demonism remains because it is fed by its own irrationality. It is based on a continuation of the anxiety of primitive man in the face of his overwhelming world; the megamachine tries to generate enough power to overcome basic human helplessness. But now we see the costs of the lie: the users of the megamachine are led into a megalomanic and paranoid distortion of reality. Once you start an arms race, you are consumed by it. This is the tragic fatality of power, that it leads to a fundamental distortion of the reality of man's relationship to nature—and so can undermine his own well-being. To protect himself with his megamachines, man is willing to sacrifice almost everything else. This is why the mega-machine represents the major historical challenge facing western man; to see through it and get control of it is the focal problem of human survival in our time.[6]

Thus Mumford's philosophy of the obscenity of history that he has pulled together with such a masterful sweep; it is both Marxist and psychological, which is what gives it its explanatory power. I am lingering on it for two reasons. For one thing it beautifully sums up and puts into focus what is already an agreed-on reading of the evolution of the destructive power of the state. For another thing, I find fault with Mumford's presentation: he leaves us a bit suspended, somehow failing to convince us of the necessary serious-ness of the whole process; he seems to gloss over the irrational dynamics of history even while talking about them. My point is, I think, that his thesis is still too Marxian and unpsychological; and this has to be remedied.

The clue to my disappointment is contained in statements like these: "Perhaps the most mysterious of all human institutions, one that has been often described but never adequately explained, is that of human sacrifice: a magical effort either to expiate guilt or promote a more abundant yield of crops." "Among the cultivated Maya, slaves were even sacrificed at an upper-class feast, merely to give it a properly genteel elegance." Or, again, "the primary motivation, in the case of human sacrifices, with its many grades from finger joints to whole bodies, [is] unexplained, and perhaps, like other irrationalities, unexplainable."[7] Now the first of these three statements is too glib, the second superficial, and the third erroneous; this is a serious matter for a philosophy of history *based on* the phenomenon of sacrifice, and needs to be remedied; only by being completely clear about sacrifice can we get a truly subtle picture of historical demonism.

The Mystery of Sacrifice

Alex Comfort once observed very aptly that the whole meaning of the Freudian revolution in thought was that it revealed to us that *the irrational had structure* and so we could begin to understand it. Mumford has evidently not fully integrated the psychoanalytic contribution into his thought if he claims that irrationalities are unexplanable. Furthermore, sacrifice *has* been adequately explained on its many levels of meaning, so fortunately we need not go into them all here.[8] Let us just say a few things about sacrifice on its most basic level, where it reveals its essential meaning. At this level sacrifice is what Mumford said it was: an admission of the pitiful finitude and powerlessness of man in the face of the *mysterium tremendum* of the universe, the immensity of what transcends him and negates his significance. At this level sacrifice affirms *reality*, bows to it, and attempts to conciliate it. Sacrifice, then, is not an "irrational aberration," but a basic human reflex of *truth*, a correct expiation of natural guilt. One basic motive of society, as Brown said, is the symbolic expiation of guilt, which we saw as a very complex phenomenon grounded in the truth of the human condition. Guilt is one of the serious motives of man, not to be tossed off as lightly as Mumford does in the above quotes from a book in which the word does not even appear in the index.

If we are to understand the happenings of history, these happenings have to be seen as resulting from the *composite* of human motives, not simply from the aberrations of power or the elusiveness of a dream. Mumford tells us that the new technology and the promise of abundance were the dream that kept mankind mesmerized; he says too that the oppressiveness of tyranny would not have been tolerated but for the positive goods that flowed out of the megamachines.[9] But people bear tyranny because of its rewards not only to their stomachs but also to their souls. They support tyranny by willingly marching off to war not only because that reduces the frustration they feel at home toward authority, not only because it enables them to project their hatreds on the enemy, but also because it expiates *their guilt*. How else explain the parents that we read about during each war who, when told about the tragic death of their son, have expressed regret that they had not more to give? This is the age-old essence of primitive gift giving; it chills us only by the nature of the sacrifice that they make so willingly and by the secondhand god to whom it is offered—the nation-state.[10] But it is not cynical or callous: in guilt one gives with a melting heart and with choking tears because one *is* guilty, one is transcended by the unspeakable majesty and superlativeness of the natural and cultural world, against which one feels realistically humbled; by giving one draws oneself into that power and merges one's existence with it.

Furthermore—and this takes us deeper into the problem—sacrifice and scapegoating are not technical tricks to overcome anxiety. Mumford says that the spilling of blood, because it is a life substance, may be a magical effort to make crops grow. Of course. In one of its forms scapegoating is also magical in origin: a ritual is performed over a goat, by which all the tribe's uncleanliness (sin) is transferred to the animal; it is then driven off or killed, leaving the village clean. But we know by now that all these technical efforts are inseparably sacred ones, which means that they represent not only an arrangement of life but a real spiritual purge that qualifies one to triumph over death. I doubt that slaves were sacrificed at an upper-class feast of the Maya "merely to give it a properly genteel elegance," as Mumford would have it. It is true that primitives have often spilled blood in order simply to gloat and strut over an enemy; but I think the motive is more elemental than merely to give to feasts a pleasant veneer. Men spill blood because it makes their hearts glad and fills out their organisms with a sense of vital power; ceremoniously killing captives is a way of affirming power over life, and therefore over death. The sacrificer may *seem* nonchalant about it, but this is because men like to experience their power effortlessly and smoothly, as though they were accustomed by nature to dispose of the strongest force she had to offer. (Detroit car makers who sell power and speed—with their businessman's realism about the truths of life—have long known this.)

And here we have to bring up again one of the central ideas discussed in Chapter Two, when we considered the dynamics of gift giving. It relates not only to guilt but fundamentally to power. The sacrifice is a gift, a gift to the gods which is directed to the flow of power, to keeping the life force moving there where it has been blocked by sin. With the sacrifice man feeds the gods to give them more power so that he may have more. The sacred food has the strength of life. The sacrifice of living things adds visible life power to the stream of life; the more living things sacrificed, the more extravagant release of power, etc. The ancient custom of sacrificing wives, slaves, and cavaliers when a king died was not only that they should continue to serve the master in the invisible world—that was a matter of course. What they achieved by suffering and dying together as living sacrifices was to bring extravagant new life into being. The sacrifice was a means for establishing a communion with the invisible world, making a circle on the flow of power, a bridge over which it could pass. So, for example, in the simple "building sacrifice" when one took possession of a piece of ground: the sacrifice expulsed the demonic spirits in the soil and released powers that literally purged the place and made building upon it safe.[11]

Now this idea of the flux and flow of power is hard for us to understand today—or rather would be hard if we had not had some experience with it: I mean of course the psychology of the Nazi experience, which served as a grim refresher course on the metaphysics of mass slaughter. Leo Alexander, in his outstanding paper on the SS, points out how much the Nazis were animated by what he calls a "heathen concept": they had a whole philosophy of blood and soil which contained the belief that death nourishes life. This was "heathen" indeed: we recognize it as the familiar archaic idea that the sacrifice of life makes life flow more plentifully. Alexander calls the Nazi delight in death a "thanatolatry," but I would prefer to talk about a "death potlatch" by means of which death is thought to mystically replenish life. It is unmistakable in the Nazi psychology. Goering, for example, made a statement early in the war that "with every German airman who is killed by the enemy our *Luftwaffe* becomes stronger." Here are a few more choice examples of the metaphysics of the death potlatch:

Dr. Karl Brandt, plenipotentiary in charge of all medical activities in the Reich, when asked about his attitude toward the killing of human beings in the course of medical experiments, replied, "Do you think that one can obtain any worthwhile fundamental results without a definite toll of lives? The same goes for technologic development. You cannot build a great bridge, a gigantic building—you cannot establish a speed record without deaths!"

In a similar vein, many SS men took a curious pride in the fact that even in peacetime they had many fatalities during "realistic" military training. Human bodies were encased in the concrete fortifications and bunkers, as though such bodies could give strength to inanimate matter.[12]

If we understand sacrifice in both its dimensions—as guilt and as the unblocking of power—we can see how logically and unmysteriously warfare had to increase in viciousness: men staged whatever size death potlatch they were technically capable of, from Genghis Khan to Auschwitz. The general opinion is that at the most primitive level of religious organization—that of shamanism—sacrifice of war captives was a rarity; captives could be taken in small number for a variety of reasons, but usually simple sadistic ones like gloating over torture or personal ones like avenging the loss of members of one's own family.[13] And this is in accord with what we saw in Chapter Two; in simpler societies expiation for guilt was easier to achieve and required no massive expenditure of life. But as societies increased in scale and complexity, incorporating high gods, a priesthood, and a king, the motive for sacrifice became frankly one of pleasing the gods and building power, and then mountains of war captives began to be sacrificed. When much booty and many slaves were brought back from raiding expeditions, it may have seemed that the purpose was secular and economic, but it was basically religious: it was a matter of affirming one's power over life and death; and the lure of economic gain was always outweighed by the magical power of war, no matter how this was disguised. The kings of Dahomey undertook their war expeditions to bring back slaves to sell to Europeans. They held an "annual custom" at which hundreds of prisoners' heads were lopped off and placed in heaps—a celebration of victory which the king offered to the people. To the amazement of the European slave traders, the king would not sell these victims even when there was a dearth of slaves for sale; in spite of his avarice the sacrificial slaughter had to take place. The reason, of course, was that the ceremony was not economic, but sacred. The affirmation of the king's power was much more important than mere possession: power is the ability to dispense life and death for the whole tribe and in relation to all of nature.[14]

Allied to this dynamic is another one which we have trouble understanding today: the one who makes the sacrifice dispenses not only power but fate; if you kill your enemy, your life is affirmed because it proves that the gods favor you. The whole philosophy is summed up in the lines from a typical "western" movie, when the Indians come upon a cavalry officer and the leader says, "Let's see if his gods protect him—shoot!" The point we moderns miss is that this is not said out of cocky pride or cynicism, as if the Indian knew in advance that the enemy would fall: ancient man really wanted to *see*. As Huizinga pointed out, war was a test of the will of the gods, to see if they favored you; it forced a revelation of destiny and so it was a holy cause and a sacred duty, a kind of divination.[15] Whatever the outcome was, it was a decision of holy validity—the highest kind of judgment man can get—and it was in *his* hands to be able to force it: all he had to do was to stage a war. It was thus natural for the divine kings, who had total power over their people, to want to test their own fate before the highest court. It is as though they said to the gods, "Now show me if I'm really as special as I believe; prove to me that I am your favored son." With the massive slave armies spread across the plain, the flotilla of ships choking the shore, the arms glistening in the sun, and the din rising to the heavens, the divine king must have felt that a sacrifice hunt of such magnitude could not fail, that he could almost defiantly force the favor of the gods in view of the blood that would flow for them.

This was the gift complex of the primitive potlatch magnified to its highest intensity: the dialogue with the gods was there, and the sacrificial gift was prominent; the accent was on massive visible power; the ambition was to mount the biggest production possible. And so it made no difference how many were killed, or from what side they came. War was a sacred duty and a holy cause, but it was *the king's* cause: its primary meaning was to prove *his power* to survive. And so the more dead, the better. As Canetti so well put it, in a book full of remarkable insight:

Fortunate and favored, the survivor stands in the midst of the fallen. For him there is one tremendous fact; while countless others have died, many of them his comrades, he is still alive. The dead lie helpless; he stands upright amongst them, and it is as though the battle had been fought in order for him to survive it. . . . It is a feeling of being chosen from amongst the many who manifestly shared the same fate. . . . The man who achieves this often is a *hero*. He is stronger. There is more life in him. He is the favored of the Gods.[16] *

As Winston Churchill discovered in one of his first military experiences: "Nothing in life is so exhilarating as to be shot at without result." And as Hitler concluded—after miraculously surviving the bomb blast that was meant to take his life but instead took several others, "Providence has kept me alive to complete my great work."

Canetti goes on to point out, and I believe truly, that the larger and more frequent the heaps of dead which attest to one's special favor, the more one needs this confirmation. It becomes a kind of addiction to proving an ever-growing sense of invulnerability, to tasting the continually repeated pleasure of survival. If the king is victorious, then all the dead on the battlefield belong to him because they prove his specialness.[17] No wonder the divine kings repeatedly staged their compulsive campaigns and inscribed the mountainous toll of their butchery for all time. We now understand that their pride was holy; they had offered the gods an immense sacrifice and a direct challenge, and the gods had confirmed that their destiny was indeed divinely favored, since the victories went to them. In recent times Lyndon B. Johnson threw out the same challenge to God from the White House—to show His favor by giving victory. And he still used the language of the hunt: the disgusting and useless slaughter of the war in Vietnam was referred to by the President as a challenge to "bring the coon-skin home and hang it on the wall."

This homely hunting language makes it very clear to us that animal power is the driving motive behind even the most abstract

---

* Canetti is a literary man, and I am continually amazed by how much more penetrating have been the analyses by nonscientists into scientific matters than those by most of the scientists themselves. Sensitive insight and great scope are evidently not usually a matter of scientific training or disposition. Carlo Levi, also a literary man, belongs with Canetti in the deluge of modern understanding of the dynamics of large-scale butchery. See his beautiful little book *Of Fear and Freedom* (New York: Farrar Straus, 1950), so eloquent and fine, and packed with all the correct ideas on sacrifice, slavery in the ancient world, the tyranny of the state, blood sacrifice in modern warfare, etc.

viciousness of men. And how could it be otherwise? Man is an animal organism who must naturally aggress on his world in order to incorporate the energy-power he needs from it. On the most elemental level this power resides in food, which is why primitives have always acknowledged food power as the basic one in the sacrificial meal. From the beginning, man, as a meat-eating hunter, incorporated the power of other animals. But he himself was a peculiarly weak animal, and so he had to develop a special sensitivity to sources of power, and a wide latitude of sources of power for his own incorporation. This is one way to understand the greater aggressiveness of man than of other animals: he was the only animal conscious of death and decay, and so he engaged in a heightened search for powers of self-perpetuation. Any study of the early evolution of warfare and the natural viciousness of it has to take this into account. Very early in human evolution men aggressed in order to incorporate two kinds of power, physical *and* symbolic. This meant that trophy taking in itself was a principal motive for war raiding; the trophy was a personal power acquisition. Men took parts of the animals they killed in the hunt as a testimonial to their bravery and skill—buffalo horns, grizzly bear claws, jaguar teeth. In war they took back proof that they had killed an enemy, in the form of his scalp or even his whole head or whole body skin.[18] These could be worn as badges of bravery which gave prestige and social honor and inspired fear and respect. But more than that, as we saw in Chapter Two, the piece of the terrible and brave animal and the scalp of the feared enemy often contained power *in themselves:* they were magical amulets, "powerful medicine," which contained the spiritual powers of the object they belonged to. And so trophies were a major source of protective power: they shielded one from harm, and one could also use them to conjure up evil spirits and exorcise them. In addition to this the trophy was the visible proof of survivorship in the contest and thus a demonstration of the favor of the gods. What greater badge of distinction than that? No wonder trophy hunting was a driving obsession among primitives: it gave to men what they needed most —extra power over life and death. We see this most directly, of course, in the actual incorporation of parts of the enemy; in cannibalism after victory the symbolic animal makes closure on both ends of his problematic dualism—he gets physical and spiritual energy. An Associated Press dispatch from the "Cambodian Front Lines" quotes a Sgt. Danh Hun on what he did to his North Vietnamese foes:

I try to cut them open while they're still dying or soon after they are dead. That way the livers give me the strength of my enemy. . . . [One day] when they attacked we got about 80 of them and everyone ate liver.[19] *

The Logic of Scapegoating

From all this we have to agree with an observation by the existentialist Jean-Paul Sartre: "Hell is other people." From the beginning men have served the appetites of one another in the most varying ways, but these were always reducible to a single theme: the need for fuel for one's own aggrandizement and immunity. Men use one another to assure their personal victory over death. Nothing could be further from the "irrationality" that Mumford complained about. In one of the most logical formulas on the human condition Rank observed, "The death fear of the ego is lessened by the killing, the sacrifice, of the other; through the death of the other, one buys oneself free from the penalty of dying, of being killed."[20] No wonder men are addicted to war. Rank's insight is foreshadowed in

---

* There is a naturalness about trophy taking that may stem partly from man's primate nature. I am thinking of the interest that primates show for striking details and objects in their environment. Children show real fascination over gadgets and trinkets, and are constantly engaged in hoarding and swapping quantities of marbles, picture cards, etc. I remember how the agate stones that we called "moonies" seemed to possess real magical powers and how we coveted them. More than that, there may be some natural connection between trophy taking and being a hunter, oriented to a triumph over the prey. It gives a real feeling of power to bring back a part of the prey; it is a way of physically affirming one's victory. The victor does not leave the field of triumph empty-handed as he came, but actually increases his own organism as a result of the encounter, by adding to it some of the volume of the victim. A recent film study of baboons in their natural habitat showed them beating a dummy lion until its head broke off, upon which the leader seized the head and took it away with him.

the basic theory of psychoanalysis and was given by Freud him-self.[21] Freud saw that when it comes to enemies and strangers, the ego can consign them to the limbo of death without even a second thought. Modern man lives in illusion, said Freud, because he denies or suppresses his wish for the other's death and for his own immortality; and it is precisely because of this illusion that mankind cannot get control over social evils like war. This is what makes war irrational: each person has the same hidden problem, and as antag-onists obsessively work their cross purposes, the result is truly demonic; the film *The Bridge on the River Kwai* summed this up beautifully. Not only enemies but even friends and loved ones are fair fuel for our own perpetuation, said Freud: "In our unconscious we daily and hourly deport all who stand in our way, all who have offended or injured us."[22] This is the price of our natural animal narcissism; very few of us, if pressured, would be unwilling to sacrifice someone else in our place. The exception to this is of course the hero. We admire him precisely because he is willing to give his life for others instead of taking theirs for his. Heroism is an unusual reversal of routine values, and it is another thing that makes war so uplifting, as mankind has long known: war is a ritual for the emergence of heroes, and so for the transmutation of common, selfish values. In war men live their own ennoblement. But what we are reluctant to admit is that the admiration of the hero is a vicarious catharsis of our own fears, fears that are deeply hidden; and this is what plunges us into uncritical hero worship: what the hero does seems so superlative to us. Thus from another point of view we see how right Freud was on enslavement by our illusions based on our repressions.

The logic of scapegoating, then, is based on animal narcissism and hidden fear. If luck, as Aristotle said, is when the arrow hits the fellow next to you, then scapegoating is pushing the fellow into its path—with special alacrity if he is a stranger to you. A particu-larly pungent phrasing of the logic of scapegoating one's own death has been given by Alan Harrington: it is as though the sacrificer were to say to God after appraising how nature feeds voraciously on life, "If this is what you want, here, take it!"[23]—but leave *me* alone.

If anyone still thinks that this is merely clever phrasing in the minds of alienated intellectuals trying to make private sense out of the evil of their world, let him consult the daily papers. Almost every year there is a recorded sacrifice of human life in remote areas of Chile to appease the earthquake gods. There have been fifteen recent *officially reported* cases of human sacrifice in India— one being that of a four-year-old boy sacrificed to appease a Hindu goddess, and another involving a west Indian immigrant couple in England who sacrificed their 16-year-old son, following prayer and meditation, to ward off the death of the mother. Freud was right; in the narcissism of earthly bodies, where each is imprisoned fatally in his own finite integument, *everyone* is alien to oneself and subject to the status of scapegoat for one's own life.*

The logic of killing others in order to affirm our own life unlocks much that puzzles us in history, much that with our modern minds we seem unable to comprehend, such as the Roman arena games. If the killing of a captive affirms the power of your life, how much does the actual massive staging of life-and-death struggles affirm a whole society? The continual grinding sacrifice of animal and human life in the arenas was all of a piece with the repressions of a society that was dedicated to war and that lived in the teeth of death. It was a perfect pastime to work off anxieties and show the ultimate personal control of death: the thumbs up or thumbs down on the gladiators. The more death you saw unfold before your eyes and the more you thrust your thumbs downward, the more you bought off your own life. And why was the crucifixion such a favorite form of execution? Because, I think, it was actually a controlled *display* of dying; the small seat on the cross held the body up so that dying would be prolonged. The longer people looked at the death of someone else, the more pleasure they could have in sensing the security and the good fortune of their own survival.[24] The whole meaning of a victory celebration, as Canetti argued, is that we experience the power of our lives and the visible decrease

* Canetti speculates beautifully on how sacrifice springs from crowd fear, the same kind of fear a herd of gazelles experiences when the cheetah is chasing it: the moment of catharsis for the herd is when the fear abates because the cheetah has singled out *one* for a kill. The sacrifice of one for the many is thus a kind of natural appeasement of hostile powers. See Elias Canetti, *Crowds and Power* (London: Gollancz, 1962), p. 309.

of the enemy: it is a sort of staging of the whole meaning of a war, the demonstration of the essence of it—which is why the public display, humiliation, and execution of prisoners is so important. "They are weak and die: we are strong and live." The Roman arena games were, in this sense, a continued staging of victory even in the absence of a war; each civilian experienced the same powers that he otherwise had to earn in war.[25] If we are repulsed by the bloodthirstiness of those games, it is because we choose to banish from our consciousness what true *excitement* is. For man, maximum excitement is the confrontation of death and the skillful defiance of it by watching others fed to it as he survives transfixed with rapture. Today only those such as racing-car drivers and sports parachutists can stage these kinds of dramas in civilian life.

It seems that the Nazis really began to dedicate themselves to their large-scale sacrifices of life after 1941 when they were *beginning to lose* and suspected at some dim level of awareness that they might. They hastened the infamous "final solution" of the Jews toward the closing days of their power, and executed their own political prisoners—like Dietrich Bonhoeffer—literally moments before the end. Retreating Germans in Russia and Italy were especially apt to kill with no apparent motive, just to leave a heap of bodies. It is obvious they were offering last-minute hostages to death, stubbornly affirming in a blind, organismic way, "I will not die, you will—see?" It seems that they wanted some kind of victory over evil, and when it couldn't be the Russians, then it would be the Jews and even other Germans; any substitute scapegoat would have to do. In the recent Bengali revolt the Western Pakistanis often killed anyone they saw, and when they didn't see anyone they would throw grenades into houses; they piled up a toll of over 3 million despised Bengalis. It is obvious that man kills to *cleanse* the earth of tainted ones, and that is what victory means and how it commemorates his life and power: man is bloodthirsty to ward off the flow of his own blood. And it seems further, out of the war experiences of recent times, when man sees that he is trapped and excluded from longer earthly duration, he says, "If I can't have it, then neither can you."

Other things that we have found hard to understand have been hatreds and feuds between tribes and families, and continual butchery practiced for what seemed petty, prideful motives of personal honor and revenge. But the idea of sacrifice as self- preservation explains these very directly. As Rank saw, the characteristic of primitives and of family groups was that they represented a sort of soul pool of immortality-substance. If you depleted this pool by one member, you yourself became more mortal. In Rank's inspired words:

It is my opinion that this ideology offers a basis for understanding both the bitter hatreds and feuds between North American Indian tribes, and the feuds or vendettas currently practiced in many European countries. Whether it was the theft of women under exogamy, or the murder of male members of the tribe, it was always a matter of avenging serious offenses upon the *spiritual economy* of the community which, being robbed of one of its *symbols of spiritual revenue,* sought to cancel or at least avenge the shortages created in the *immortality account.*[26]

This kind of action is natural to primitives especially, who believe in the balance of nature and are careful not to overly deplete the store of life-stuff. Revenge equals the freeing of life-stuff into the common reservoir "from which it can then be reassigned," as Jordan Scher very nicely put it. In fact, he extends the primitive notion of life-stuff right up to modern society and sees it as a motive for genocidal war and even the everyday secular process of justice: the guilty one is punished in order to return his life-stuff to the community.[27]

I don't know how much of a burden of explanation we would want to put on the pool of life-stuff in modern, secular society. For one thing, we no longer believe in the balance of nature; for another, we don't often grant to others the same life quality that we have. But whether or not we believe in a steady pool of life-stuff, numbers are important to man: if we "buy off" our own death with that of others, we want to buy it off at a good price. In wartime, as Zilboorg put it:

We mourn our dead without undue depression because we are able to celebrate an equal if not greater number of deaths in the ranks of the enemy.[28]

This explains the obsessive nature of "body counting" of the enemy as well as the universal tendency to exaggerate his losses and minimize those of one's own side. People can only lie so blatantly and eagerly when their own lives are at stake; these exaggerations always seem silly to outsiders to the conflict precisely because their lives are not involved. Rank sees, correctly we now have to believe, that *all* warfare and revolutionary struggle are simply a development of feuding and vendettas, where the basic thing at stake is a dramatization of the immortality account. We couldn't understand the obsessive development of nationalism in our time—the fantastic bitterness between nations, the unquestioned loyalty to one's own, the consuming wars fought in the name of the fatherland or the motherland—unless we saw it in this light. "Our nation" and its "allies" represent those who qualify for eternal survival; we are the "chosen people." From the time when the Athenians exterminated the Melians because they would not ally with them in war to the modern extermination of the Vietnamese, the dynamic has been the same: all those who join together under one banner are alike and so qualify for the privilege of immortality; all those who are different and outside that banner are excluded from the blessings of eternity.[29] The vicious sadism of war is not only a testing of God's favor to our side, it is also a proof that the enemy *is* mortal: "Look how we kill him." As Alan Harrington so well put it, in a remarkable book which contains the most brilliantly pungent phrasings of (Rankian) insights that one is ever likely to see:

Cruelty can arise from the aesthetic outrage we sometimes feel in the presence of strange individuals who seem to be making out all right. . . . Have they found some secret passage to eternal life? It can't be. If those weird individuals with beards and funny hats are acceptable, then what about my claim to superiority? Can someone like that be my equal in God's eyes? Does he, that one, dare hope to live forever too—and perhaps crowd me out? I don't like it. All I know is, if he's right I'm wrong. So different and funny-looking. I think he's trying to fool the gods with his sly ways. Let's show him up. He's not very strong. For a start, see what he'll do when I poke him.[30]

Sadism naturally absorbs the fear of death, as Zilboorg points out, because by actively manipulating and hating we keep our organism absorbed in the outside world; this keeps self-reflection and the fear of death in a state of low tension. We feel we are masters over life and death when we hold the fate of others in our hands. As long as we can continue shooting, we think more of killing than of being killed. Or, as a wise gangster once put it in a movie, "When killers stop killing they get killed."

This is already the essence of a theory of sadism. But more than that it is the clinical proof of the natural "wisdom" of tyrannical leaders from the time of the divine kingships up to the present day. In times of peace, without an external enemy, the fear that feeds war tends to find its outlet *within* the society, in the hatred between classes and races, in the everyday violence of crime, of automobile accidents, and even the self-violence of suicide.[31] War sucks much of this up into one fulcrum and shoots it outward to make an unknown enemy pay for our internal sins. It is as Mumford said, but—one final time—how rational this "irrationality."

The Science of Man after Hitler

It should already be obvious that with observations like these on sacrifice and scapegoating we are taking in immense areas in human relations; when we think in these terms, we already feel quickened in our thoughts and our pulse—we know we are onto something big. I have lingered on guilt, sacrifice, heroism, and immortality because they are the key concepts for the science of man in society that is emerging in our time. And the key works for these concepts have already been written, which is good news in the life of any aspiring science; the only rub is that the scientific community itself has not realized this good news, and so we have been painfully slow in forging an agreed science of man. The application of the ideas of guilt and sacrifice to modern sociology has been done largely by a few men—notably Kenneth Burke and Hugh Dalziel Duncan. Let us dwell on this critical chapter in the evolution of an authentic science of man.

Burke recognized that guilt and expiation were fundamental categories of sociological explanation, and he proposed a simple formula: guilt must be canceled in society, and it is absolved by "victimage." So universal and regular is the dynamic that Burke wondered "whether human society could possibly cohere without symbolic victims which the individual members of the group share in common." He saw "the civic enactment of redemption through the sacrificial victim" as the center of man's social motivation.[32]

Burke was led to the central idea of victimage and redemption through Greek tragedy and Christianity; he saw that this funda- mentally religious notion is a basic characteristic of any social order. Again we are brought back to our initial point that all culture is in essence sacred—*supernatural*, as Rank put it. The miraculous- ness of creation is after all magnified in social life; it is contained in persons and given color, form, drama. The natural mystery of birth, growth, consciousness, and death is taken over by society; and as Duncan so well says, this interweaving of social form and natural terror becomes an inextricable *mystification;* the individual can only gape in awe and guilt.[33] This religious guilt, then, is also a charac- teristic of so-called secular societies; and anyone who would lead a society must provide for some form of sacred absolution, regard- less of the particular historical disguise that this absolution may wear. Otherwise society is not possible. In Burke's generation it was above all Hitler, Stalin, and Mussolini who understood this and acted on it.

If there is one thing that the tragic wars of our time have taught us, it is that the enemy has a ritual role to play, by means of which evil is redeemed. All "wars are conducted as 'holy' wars"[34] in a double sense then—as a revelation of fate, a testing of divine favor, *and* as a means of purging evil from the world at the same time. This explains why we are dedicated to war precisely in its most horrifying aspects: it is a passion of human purgation. Nietzsche observed that "whoever is dissatisfied with himself is always ready to revenge himself therefore; we others will be his victims. . . ."[35] But the irony is that men are always dissatisfied and guilty in small and large ways, and this is what drives them to a search for purity where all dissatisfaction can come to a head and be wiped away. Men try to qualify for eternalization by being clean and by cleans- ing the world around them of the evil, the dirty; in this way they show that they are on the side of purity, even if they themselves

are impure. The striving for perfection reflects man's effort to get
some human grip on his eligibility for immortality. And he can
only know if he is good if the authorities tell him so; this is why
it is so vital for him emotionally to know whether he is liked or
disliked, why he will do anything the group wants in order to
meet its standards of "good": his eternal life depends on it.[36] Good
and bad relate to strength and weakness, to self-perpetuation, to
indefinite duration. And so we can understand that all ideology, as
Rank said, is about one's qualification for eternity; and so are all
disputes about who really is dirty. The target of one's righteous
hatred is always called "dirt"; in our day the short-hairs call the
long-hairs "filthy" and are called in turn "pigs." Since everyone
feels dissatisfied with himself (dirty), victimage is a universal human need. And the highest heroism is the stamping out of those
who are tainted. The logic is terrifying. The psychoanalytic group-
ing of guilt, anality, and sadism is translatable in this way to the
highest levels of human striving and to the age-old problem of good
and evil.

From which we have to conclude that men have been the mid-
wives of horror on this planet because this horror alone gave them
peace of mind, made them "right" with the world. No wonder
Nietzsche would talk about "the disease called man."[37] It seems
perverse when we put it so blatantly, yet here is an animal who
needs the spectacle of death in order to open himself to love. As
Duncan put it:

. . . as we wound and kill our enemy in the field and slaughter his
women and children in their homes, our love for each other deepens. We
become comrades in arms; our hatred of each other is being purged in
the sufferings of our enemy.[38]

And even more relentlessly:

We *need* to socialize in hate and death, as well as in joy and love. We
do not know how to have friends without, at the same time, creating
victims whom we must wound, torture, and kill. Our love rests on hate.[39]

If we talk again and shockingly about human baseness, it is
not out of cynicism; it is only to better get some kind of factual

purchase on our fate. We follow Freud in the belief that it is only illusions that we have to fear; and we follow Hardy—in our epigraph to this book—in holding that we have to take a full look at the worst in order to begin to get rid of illusions. Realism, even brutal, is not cynicism. As Duncan so passionately concluded his Nietzschean and Dostoevskian exposition of the terrifying dynamics of purity and love, ". . . we cannot become humane until we understand our need to visit suffering and death on others. . . . The sociology of our time must begin in [such an] anguished awareness. . . ."[40] It has already begun in the work of Burke, Duncan, Mumford, and Lifton; but its theoretical formulations were already plentifully contained in the neglected work of Rank. From the point of view of such a sociology, the great scientific problems of our time have been the successful and grand social cohesions, especially of Hitler, Stalin, and Mao. Burke and Duncan have amply described the religious horror drama of Germany under Hitler, where the dirty and evil Jews were purged from the world of Aryan purity by the Nazi priesthood.[41] Buchenwald and Auschwitz were the result of one of the most massive mystifications of history, a religious use of man's fundamental motives and fears. Today we still gape in unbelief that such a holocaust was possible in our "civilized" world, refusing to see how true it was to man's nature and to his ambitions to transcend that nature. Hitler's rise to power was based on his understanding of what people wanted and needed most of all, and so he promised them, above everything else, *heroic victory over evil;* and he gave them the living possibility of ridding themselves temporarily of their real guilt. As many die-hard rightists in the U.S. today realize better than anyone else, the tragedy of Vietnam is that it has loaded the Americans with a huge burden of unresolvable guilt and it has not been a victory. They rightly say that leaders who saddle a nation with such a bafflement of its true aspirations have no right to lead. The nation represents victory and immortality or it has no mandate to exist. It must give tangible, straightforward victories or its credit is dissipated in the hearts of all its citizens. The rightists rally behind the convicted war criminal Lieut. William Calley because they cannot stand the burden of guilt of a nonvictorious war, so they simply deny it by insisting that he is a straightforward hero. There is no immortality without guiltless victory. On these matters rightists have always been a candid barometer of basic human urges.

It took Stalin's purge trials to show us that the highest humanistic ideals of socialist revolutionaries also have to be played out in a religious drama of victimage and redemption—if one is to have a pure and cohesive socialist society at all.[42] The Russians exiled religious expiation but could not exile their own human nature, and so they had to conjure up a secular caricature of religious expiation. And they are still doing it: the magician-priests who give absolution to the clean communist masses now wear the white coats of hospital psychiatrists who transform dirty dissident victims with the latest techniques of "secular" science. It is grotesque, but Burke had warned us to always watch for the "secular equivalents" of the theological formula of victimage and redemption; the scapegoat is not a " 'necessary illusion' of savages, children, and the masses,"[43] but now an achievement of the "most advanced" socialist society.

Most recently Robert Jay Lifton has extended the Rankian framework of analysis into a brilliant dissection of that other great socialist drama of redemption of our time—the one staged by Mao, the biggest drama of all to date, yet one that uses the same time-honored dynamics. Lifton's analysis reveals Maoism as still another version of age-old historical themes dating from the time of the emergence of the very first states. Here is a reenactment of the drama of cosmic government, with Mao as the god-king who channels sacred power to those on the side of purity and right. Those who are not on that side fit into the now familiar formula of "victimization . . . the need to reassert one's own immortality, or that of one's group, by contrasting it with its absolute absence [of immortality] in one's death-tainted victim."[44] Mao emerges as a hero-savior who has the particular skill of defying death and giving expiation to his followers—"a man closely attuned to the pulse of immortality," as Lifton put it.[45] The vehicle for immortality is, of course, the revolution itself, the noble mission of the Chinese masses, the mission into which one merges his entire identity and from which he receives his apotheosis. In this cosmology it is the people themselves who carry the "immortal revolutionary substance"; God, then, "is none other than the masses of the Chinese people." It is as though China herself and her staggering population had the life power to be immune to the normal limitations of human existence.[46] From Lifton's analysis it seems that modern China is reliving the idea of the primitive group soul which is a sacred fount of regeneration on which the whole community can draw so long as it remains pure. If one imagines these analogies far-fetched, he should go to Lifton himself and see how firmly they rest on a now well-founded tradition of social and psychological analysis.[47]

The Two Sides of Heroic Self-Expansion

In all this we see the continuity of history; each heroic apotheosis is a variation on basic themes because man is still man. Civilization, the rise of the state, kingship, the universal religions—all are fed by the same psychological dynamic: guilt and the need for redemption. If it is no longer the clan that represents the collective immortality pool, then it is the state, the nation, the revolutionary cell, the corporation, the scientific society, one's own race. Man still gropes for transcendence, but now this is not necessarily nature and God, but the SS or the CIA; the only thing that remains constant is that the individual still gives himself with the same humble trembling as the primitive to his totemic ancestor. The stake is identical—immortality power—and the unit of motivation is still the single individual and his fears and hopes. To see graphically how constant these things have remained, we have only to tune in on the early-morning sign-offs on American television. The message is striking in its primitiveness: several minutes of the alternation of a picture of the flag with that of soldiers in landing barges, combat aircraft streaking across the sky, soldiers marching, the green fields and hills of home, a glistening white military cemetary, again the flag unfurled in the wind, the timeless Lincoln Memorial, and again the firm and determined faces of soldiers marching. The unspoken text is relentless in its assurance of vital power to each person, and a firm place in an immortality system. How the heart must quicken at what is suggested by these images, how the throat must choke up with gratitude.

Of course militarism and the flag hardly begin to cover the various types of things that the person can expand into; human ingenuity is not so limited, which explains why rich and imaginative people often make such poor patriots. Samuel Johnson saw this clearly when he said that patriotism was the last refuge for scoundrels. In our time the young are turning to forms of what Lifton called "experiential transcendence"—the intense experience of a feeling state which, for a little while anyway, eliminates the problem of time and death.[48] This is a variation on the historical mode of mysticism, only in our time people can imbibe in it *en masse,* helped by the modern technology of color and sound. Alan Harrington caught the mood of it beautifully:

By embracing the Primordial Oneness I escape death before it can hit me. How can that shadowy menace keep an appointment in Samara with a man whose consciousness has already been dissolved? . . . In a discotheque, the careworn self is smashed by echoing guitars and electronic shrieking, and its fragments are scattered even more finely by showering and splitting light effects. . . . The narcotic drift will take you to spaces beyond time and death, as will an orgy or a church organ.[49]

This explains the massive attendance at rock music festivals which the older generation has such trouble understanding. The festivals represent a joyful triumph over the flat emptiness of modern life, the mechanical succession of news events which carry everyone on willy-nilly, the ticking away of life in an absurd anarchy. The festival is the attempt by the young to reawaken a sense of the awesome and the miraculous as they throb in full communion to the beating of the music. As one rock music authority so well put it, what the modern young are seeking through this is a way to adequately express wonder, an expression that modern, secular, mechanistic society has denied them. This kind of communion in joy and in intensive experience is, we have to conclude, modern youth's heroic victory over human limitation. Yet it, too, is hardly a modern invention despite the new technics which mediates it. It is a replay of the basic Dionysian expansiveness, the submergence and loss of identity in the transcending power of the pulsating "now" and the frenzied group of like-minded believers.

My point is that heroic expansiveness, joy, and wonder have an underside—finitude, guilt, and death—and we have to watch for its expression too. After you have melted your identity into transcending, pulsating power, what do you do to establish some kind of balance? What kind of forceful, instrumental attitude do you summon up to remarshal yourself and your grip on experience? One cannot live in the trembling smallness of awe, else he will melt away. Where is the object on which to focus one's new self-assertion—an object that is for most people a victim? This is what we have to be constantly on guard for. The Dionysian festival reflected man's experience in the round, and so for the masochistic loss of self there was the corresponding sadistic affirmation of self: the Dionysian celebrators tore apart with their bare hands and ate raw a scapegoat or a bull to climax the ceremony. Every heroic victory is two-sided: it aims toward merger with an absolute "beyond" in a burst of life affirmation, but it carries within it the rotten core of death denial in a physical body here on earth. If culture is a lie about the possibilities of victory over death, then that lie must somehow take its toll of life, no matter how colorful and expansive the celebration of joyful victory may seem. The massive meetings of the Nazi youth or those of Stalin in Red Square and Mao in Peking literally take our breath away and give us a sense of wonder. But the proof that these celebrations have an underside is in Auschwitz and Siberia: these are the places where the goats are torn apart, where the pathetic cowardliness of what it is all about on its underside is revealed. We might say that modern heroism is somewhat out of joint compared with Dionysianism, where both aspects of transcendence took place on the spot; modern scapegoating has its consummation in bureaucratic forms, gas ovens, slow rotting in prison camps. But it still is all about the real, lived terror of the individual German, Russian, and Chinese over his own life, however coldly and matter-of-factly it may be staged, whatever the clean and disinterested scientific methods used. Hannah Arendt in her brilliant and controversial analysis of Adolf Eichmann showed that he was a simple bureaucratic trimmer who followed orders because he wanted to be liked; but this can only be the surface of the story, we now see. Rubber-stampers sign orders for butchery in order to be liked; but to be liked means to be admitted to the group that is elected for immortality. The ease and remoteness of modern killing by bespectacled, colorless men seem to make it a disinterested bureaucratic matter, but evil is not banal as Arendt claimed: evil rests on the passionate person motive to perpetuate oneself, and for each individual this is literally a life-and-death matter for which any sacrifice is not too great, provided it is the sacrifice of someone else and provided that the leader and the group approve of it.

Whatever side of heroism we look at, one thing is certain: it is an all-consuming activity to make the world conform to our desires. And as far as means are concerned, we are all equally insignificant and impotent animals trying to coerce the universe, trying to make the world over to our own urges. The cultural lie merely continues and supports the lie of the Oedipal *causa sui* project*; when it is exposed, we literally become impotent. From which we can conclude that man is an animal who has to live in a lie in order to live at all. Psychiatrists who practice in New York report that the complaints of impotency increase when the stock market is in a low. Conversely, potency is vigorous when the market is high, or a "bull" market as the apt term has it. We are reminded of how archaic man quickly killed the king as soon as he became impotent: it is conceivable that for primitives, like Wall Streeters, actual impotency might develop if the cultural system of denial lost its power. All of which supports those who hold that death anxiety always lingers under the surface and is never surely and smoothly absorbed in the cultural hero system. How can the body ever be surely transcended by an animal who is body and maybe *nothing but* body and who fears this very thing on some level of his awareness?

I mention these things in passing only to remind the reader of the tragic aspect of human heroics and the naturalness of vicious scapegoating: somebody has to pay for the way things are. This is the meaning of the Devil in history, as many authorities have told us. The Devil represents the body, the absolute determinism of man's earthly condition, and that's why the Devil is so dangerous:

---

* For an elaboration of the *causa sui* project see *The Denial of Death* (New York: The Free Press, 1973).

he reveals the reality of our situation, the fact that we can't really escape our earthly destiny.[50] To fight the Devil is to fight what he stands for, and to make the Devil a scapegoat is to do away with what he represents: the defeat of the supernatural, the negation of the spiritual victory over body-boundedness. Hence all the vampire stories where the blood-feasting evil one is the terrifying threat. The truth of the vampire story, of bats, blood, and canine teeth, is the same as the truth of the castration complex: that the *causa sui* project via the body is a lie, that our bodies are really our doom; so long as we are in them we are subject to the complete dominion of earthly laws of blood and animality. Hence only the sign of the cross can win out over the vampire, only the domain of invisible spirit that promises victory over the body and death can save man. Thus the vampire story is a perennial horror-passion play reflecting the entire truth of the human condition and the hope beyond it. Hence, too, the gory stories throughout history about the Jews' appetite for Gentile children, etc.; for the Nazis the Jews were devils, just as Mao's adversaries were for him.[51] The Devil is the one who prevents the heroic victory of immortality in each culture— even the atheistic, scientific-humanist ones. On matters of spiritual apotheosis every leader shows his basic kinship to Martin Luther, because he has to decry the fettering of man's glorious spirit by the body, by personal appetite and selfishness. As Lifton so aptly points out, Mao, in his scatological lyricism (denouncing of the Chinese government's subservience to the West), reminds one precisely of Luther: "If one of our foreign masters farts, it's a lovely perfume."[52] The Devil always confounds the body with the ethereal and makes the decadent capitalist world seem like socialist heaven.

Conclusion: Cultures as Styles of Heroic Death Denial

It is fairly easy to draw the moral from all this, even though it will be shocking to some of the older styles of doing social theory. The continuity from the Enlightenment through Marx, Weber, Mannheim, Veblen, and Mills is all there plain as day. The important thing about the analyses of Rank, Burke, Duncan, and Lifton is that they reveal precisely those *secular* forms which the traditional religious dramas of redemption now take. It would be easy to argue that we now have a fairly good working catalogue of the general range of social expressions of basic human motives, and that this represents the completion of the work of the great Max Weber, who had already shown the social dramas of several historical societies, both eastern and western, in the round.

But with our greater and even more tragic historical experience which includes Hitler and Stalin, we can give the Weberian tradition even more life and critical force: we can extend it from primitive man right up to the modern revolutionary monoliths, all the while basing it on a few universal principles of human motivation. Since there is no secular way to resolve the primal mystery of life and death, all secular societies are lies. And since there is no sure human answer to such a mystery, all religious integrations are mystifications. This is the sober conclusion to which we seem to be led. *Each society is a hero system which promises victory over evil and death.* But no mortal, nor even a group of as many as 700 million clean revolutionary mortals, can keep such a promise: no matter how loudly or how artfully he protests or they protest, it is not within man's means to triumph over evil and death. For secular societies the thing is ridiculous: what can "victory" mean secularly? And for religious societies victory is part of a blind and trusting belief in another dimension of reality. Each historical society, then, is a hopeful mystification or a determined lie.

Many religionists have lamented the great toll that the Hitlers and the Stalins have taken in order to give their followers the equivalent of religious expiation and immortality; it seemed that when man lost the frank religious dimension of experience, he became even more desperate and wild; when he tried to make the earth alone a pure paradise, he had to become even more demonic and devilish. But when one looks at the toll of scapegoats that religious integrations have taken, one can agree with Duncan that religious mystifications have so far been as dangerous as any other.[53] No world view has a claim on secure truth, much less on greater purity—at least as it has been practiced historically in the social world. Harrington, as usual, sums it up very colorfully:

The plotters of earthly and heavenly paradise have fought, slandered and sabotaged one another for hundreds of years. One stands accused of un-bridled hubris (risking divine retaliation, jeopardizing everybody's chances); the other of superstition (cringing before mystery); and each finds the other obstructing the road to eternal life.[54]

Dostoevsky thought that the only hope for Russia was to worship the body of Christ and to have a contented peasantry. When we look at the toll of Stalinism we may feel wistful, but we would have to be able to count the toll of Dostoevsky's solution and then compare. We don't have to get embroiled in any abstract arguments because the shape of social theory is clear. If each historical society is in some ways a lie or a mystification, the study of society becomes *the revelation of the lie.* The comparative study of society becomes *the assessment of how high are the costs of this lie.* Or, looked at from another way, cultures are fundamentally and basically *styles of heroic death denial.* We can then ask empirically, it seems to me, what are the costs of such denials of death, because we know how these denials are structured into styles of life.* These costs can be tallied roughly in two ways: in terms of the tyranny practiced within the society, and in terms of the victimage practiced against aliens or "enemies" outside it.[55]

By assessing the cost of scapegoating and by trying to plan for alternative ideals that will absorb basic human fears, we seem to have brought up to date the Marxist critique of the human eva-sion of freedom; we seem to have finally a secure grip on the social problem of death denial. In the Marxist view death is an ideology, as the title of an essay by Marcuse has it. This means that although death is a natural fear, this fear has always been used and exploited by the established powers in order to secure their domination. Death is a "culture mechanism" that was utilized by societies from primitive times on as a means of social control and repression, to help an elite enforce its will on a meek and

---

* Franz Borkenau talks about cultures as death-denying, death-defying, and death-accepting, alternating with each other in history. But this kind of classi-fication seems to me to refer more to different types of transcendence; one still has to ask how self-perpetuation is secured in each culture—at least for the masses, if not for the few intellectual formulators. See his "The Concept of Death," *The Twentieth Century,* 1955, 157:317.

compliant populace. The definition of culture, after all, is that it continues the *causa sui* project of the transcendence of death; and so we see the fatality and naturalness of human slavishness: man helps secure his own domination by the tribe, the polis, the state, the gods, because of his fears.[56]

When we phrase the problem in these terms, we can see how immense it is and how far it extends beyond our traditional ways of doing science. If you talk about heroics that cost mountains of human life, you have to find out why such heroics are practiced in a given social system: who is scapegoating whom, what social classes are excluded from heroism, what there is in the social structure that drives the society blindly to self-destructive heroics, etc. Not only that, but you have to actually set up some kind of liberating ideal, some kind of life-giving alternative to the thoughtless and destructive heroism; you have to begin to scheme to give to man an opportunity for heroic victory that is not a simple reflex of narcissistic scapegoating. You have to conceive of the possibility of a nondestructive *yet victorious* social system. It was precisely this problem that was designed by William James over two generations ago, in his famous essay "The Moral Equivalent of War," but needless to say we have done nothing about it even on a conceptual level, much less on an active social level. Little wonder that things are in a mess.

One of the reasons social scientists have been slow in getting around to such designs has been the lack of an adequate and agreed general theory of human nature. James didn't have one, and it has taken us this long to begin to sort out the real legacy of Freud. Modern Marxism still does not show man in the round and so still seems naive to mature scholars in its easy optimism. Even the injection of Freudian dogma into Marxism, in the work of Marcuse, is still too clumsy a commentary on the human condition. I will sum up a critique of Marcuse toward the close of this book; but right now it is important to direct the reader in the quest for an agreed general theory of human nature to *exactly what cripples the autonomy of the individual.* The Enlightenment hope for free and autonomous men was never born; and one reason is that we have not known until after Freud the precise dynamics that makes men so tragically slavish. Why are all enjoinders to us to take command of our fears, to stand upright, to build a science in society that reflects rational control—why are these so impossibly utopian? We have already in this book seen most of the reasons for this. It remains now to put the last technical piece into place. This should enable us to finally piece together the legacy of Freud for social science.

Transference

Freud saw that the patient in analysis developed intense attachment to the person of the analyst. The analyst became the core of his life, the object of his every thought, a complete fascination. Seeing that this was an uncanny phenomenon, Freud explained it as transference—that is, the transference of feelings the patient once had towards his parents to the new power figure in his life, the doctor. Expanding his findings into a theoretical framework using transference as a universal mechanism, Freud directed his interests to the psychology of leadership and produced his *Group Psychology and the Analysis of the Ego*. Here, in less than 100 pages, he explained why men were so sheeplike when they functioned in groups—how they abandoned their egos to the leader, identified with his powers just as they did once before when as dependent children they yielded to their parents.

Gradually, through the works of Adler, Rank, Fromm, Jung, and others, we have seen a shift in emphasis to a more comprehensive view of transference, building on Freud. So that today we can say that transference is a reflex of the fatality of the human condition. Transference to a powerful other takes care of the overwhelmingness of the universe. Transference to a powerful other handles the fear of life and death. To avoid repetition of myself, I refer the interested reader to "The Spell Cast by Persons," a complete chapter on transference in *The Denial of Death*.

CHAPTER NINE

Social Theory:
The Merger of Marx and Freud

Let us take a lingering look over our shoulder to see where we have come. Rousseau, as we saw in Chapter Three, made an important beginning in trying to explain the problems we have been dealing with in the last five chapters—how oppression, degradation, and large-scale misery and evil arose out of a relatively harmless primitive human state. But Rousseau's thesis, like that of traditional Marxist theory, does not take sufficient account of the psychological dimension of man's unfreedom. This we will take up further in this chapter, and we will place the psychological aspect right where it belongs: at the heart of social theory.

Conservatives, who never took Rousseau seriously except as a madman, never agreed with Marxian theory either. As Edmund Burke and others who shuddered at the French Revolution understood, it still left human nature intact, and so had to again bring about a relatively deplorable and tragic state of affairs. There was a long current of disagreement in the nineteenth century about many aspects of Marx's theory about primitive communism, about the origin of the state in conquest, etc., but it all came to rest on one problem alone: the nature of man. The Marxists thought that man was unfree because he was coerced by the power of others; the conservatives said he was unfree because of innate differences in men. Some men worked harder, some were stronger, some had more talent and skill, hence things were naturally unequal. People needed to work together, to make and gather the fruits of uneven talents, and so society by its nature was a necessary and willing agreement to share unequally among unequals. If inequalities were greater in modern times, well, so were the fruits which most people could enjoy; greater, too, were the differences in skill, etc. So the conservatives were relatively free of the moral outrage and sense of injustice which animated the radicals and still animates them. But they themselves were profoundly outraged by the cost in human lives and misery of the revolutions that were supposed to set things straight, and that only seemed to make man as much of a slave and a cipher as he was before, if not more so. In czarist times a political prisoner might bribe a jailer, but in Soviet Russia today no dissenter can bribe the white-frocked state psychiatrist out of plugging him into the wall.

If we shudder at the thought of the total determinism of modern tyranny, we must admit that the conservative case has weight, just as it had in the nineteenth century, especially since we today know fairly accurately how historical inequality came about—at least in a theoretical way. And we know that this process started long before the rise of the state: in fact, it was inherent in primitive societies themselves, as we saw in Chapter Three—even in the most egalitarian ones, in hunting and gathering societies, the simplest known. These societies knew no distinctions of rank, little or no authority of one individual over another; they had very simple possessions and so there was no real difference in wealth; property was distributed equally. Yet even on this level individual differences were recognized and already formed the germ of social differentiation which would gradually lead to distinctions of rank, accumulated wealth, hereditary privilege, and the eventual rise and entrenchment of the exploitative state.

To return to our discussion of Rousseau in Chapter Three, it would seem that, with its emphasis on differences in personal qualities as the largest factor in inequality among men, his "Discourse"[1] *supports* the conservative argument—or would support it, rather, if the essay were not filled with errors and fantastic conjectures. I am not going to burden the reader with an assessment of Rousseau's essay, picking out its brilliant insights or its ludicrous ones based on a fanciful anthropology, but will only cite two crucial points. First, the basic fallacy: that there was a time in early social evolution when men were not influenced by differences in personal qualities. Rousseau is able to maintain this because of a truly fantastic sketch of social evolution, in which he sees man at first as an isolated animal, not even living in a family group. Gradually family life evolved, and then tribal life, and it was at that time that "each one began to look at the others and to want to be looked at himself, and public esteem had a value."[2] His famous idea on the "state of nature" begins, then, with the epoch of the "savage" who "lives within himself." It ends when man came out of this state into that of society; he became "sociable man, always outside himself," who "knows how to live only in the opinion of others." And so Rousseau can conclude that man's downfall does not begin in the "original state of man," but "that it is the spirit of society alone, and the inequality it engenders, which thus change and alter all our natural inclinations"[3]—that is, our "natural" solitariness, our "natural immunity" to the personal qualities of others.*

The second point of fantasy in Rousseau's essay is easier to understand because it is based on fact: he saw no accumulation of goods in the primitive societies of his time, and so he thought that primitive man wanted "only to live and remain idle" and refused to work to build up an accumulation of goods. Accumulated goods in civilized society were a visible burden on those who slaved for them, and they were a direct cause of social injustice; and so Rousseau could say that the primitive state was one of delightful laziness and freedom.[4] But we know this is the wrong conclusion: rather, hunters and gatherers cannot accumulate a surplus because of primitive technology and subsistence economy, not because they do not want the surplus. They are already eager to accumulate a surplus of wives and to gain special privileges for hunting lands,

* There is no point in confronting this thesis with the data of evolution which show that man must have always lived in some kind of family group just like his primate ancestors. Or with the data of social psychology which show that self-esteem is artificialized right from the maternal milk and the first words the child learns. Or in pointing out how conveniently blurred Rousseau's exposition is: he uses the word "savage" for those at the first stage of the state of nature and those at the last, when they are already—by his analysis— "sociable" men and hence corrupted. The Caribs that he lauds as "savages" were hardly in a state of nature, since they were already "sociable" men who knew full well about such things as "power and reputation." (Jean-Jacques Rousseau, *The First and Second Discourses*, 1755 [New York: St. Martin's, 1964], ed. R. D. Masters, p. 179.) But by this elastic use of the word "savage" Rousseau could talk about an ideal man that predates society, and he could also use the primitive societies *of his time* as an ideal criticism of his own western society. So Rousseau could blame natural inequality for causing wealth and corruption, and he could decry inequality at the same time as an artificial creation of advanced social life. In this way, he moved imperceptibly from the *psychology* of inequality to the *historical injustice* of it.

etc. The drive for self-expansion is there, but there are neither op-portunities nor the world picture into which to fit it. Or, as we would say with Brown, the state of nature is not idle, it is anal like all other human states.

Since Rousseau wrote, we have learned something from the vast collections of data on primitive man: that if he was not in bondage to the authority of living persons, he was at the utter mercy of the power of spirits. Because of man's fear of life and death, the tribe was in hock to the spirits of the dead. Or, if in some tribes men did not seem to fear death, it was because they had transmuted this fear by immersing themselves in the group ideology, whatever it may have been. Now this leads us to a completely opposite position from Rousseau, even on his fanciful sketch of social evo-lution: that is, in the state of nature the solitary individual is already *unfree*, even before he gets to society; he carries within himself the bondage that he needs in order to live. We know today that Rousseau used the idea of the "state of nature" as an explora-tory hypothesis to be able to imagine how life might be in a state of freedom from social coercion. We know too what a powerful critical tool this idea has been, and how it has helped us to high-light the state as a structure of domination from Marx all the way up to Mumford. But the fact is that man never was free and cannot be from his own nature as the *starting* point. Rare individuals may *achieve* freedom at the end of years of experience and effort, and they can do this best under conditions of advanced civilization such as those that Rousseau scorned.

As we have seen, each human type seeks to perpetuate itself if it has the power to do so; it tries to expand and aggrandize itself in the ways open to it. But on primitive levels the power figures are always suspect precisely because of their dangerous power; hence the constant anxiety about witches, etc. It was Frazer who showed that the early tribal embodiments of magical power were ready scapegoats for the people—not only witches but priest-kings too.[5] No wonder that when kings later got real power to work their will on the helpless masses, they used that power ruthlessly; in this perspective the divine king of the great slave state of the Mediterranean basin is the earlier shaman come of age and of unlimited power.[6] We might say that instead of themselves being

scapegoats, they used the entire people as their own sacrificial animals, marching them off to military holocausts at will. The logic
of this kind of turning of the tables is almost inevitable. As Canetti
has so beautifully argued, what each person wants is to be a
survivor, to cheat death and to remain standing no matter how
many others have fallen around him. In tribal society the *people*
are the survivors if they can be, even at the expense of an occasional
power figure who detaches himself too much from the general level
of safe mutuality and symbiosis. In the later tyrannical state, it
was only natural that the king reverse this procedure—that he
prove himself to be *the* survivor no matter how many of his people
died, or even *because* they died, as we saw in Chapter Eight.[7]

Seen in this way, history is the saga of the working out of one's
problems on others—harmlessly when one has no power (or when
the "weapon" is art), viciously when one has the power and when
the weapons are the arsenals of the total state. This saga continues
in modern times but in forms which disguise the coercion and
emphasize the social agreement, but the dialogue is the same: individuals skilled in focusing power, and masses hungry for it and
fearful of it. Each society elevates and rewards leaders who are
talented at giving the masses heroic victory, expiation for guilt,
relief of personal conflicts. It doesn't matter how these are achieved:
magical religious ritual, magical booming stock markets, magical
heroic fulfillment of five-year plans, or mana-charged military megamachines—or all together. What counts is to give the people the
self-expansion in righteousness that they need. The men who have
power can exercise it through many different kinds of social and
economic structures, but a universal psychological hunger underpins
them all; it is this that locks people and power figures together
in a life-and-death contract.

The Nature of Man

The question of the origins of inequality is only half of the
problem of a sophisticated Marxist philosophy of history. The other
half is that Rousseau's argument with Hobbes has never been

satisfactorily settled. The Marxists have said, with Rousseau, that human nature is a blank slate, neutral, even good; evil exists because of social institutions that encourage it, because of social classes and the hate, envy, competition, degradation, and scapegoating that stem from them; change society and man's natural goodness will flower. Not so, say the conservatives, and they point for proof at those revolutionary societies which have abolished social class but which continue to express personal and social evil; evil, then, must be in the heart of the creature; the best that social institutions can do is to keep it blunted; and social institutions that already effectively do this without excessive repression and within legal safeguards for individual rights—why, such social institutions should not be changed. So argue the conservatives.

This question has been the central one of the science of man, and as such the knottiest in its whole career; thus it is logical that it is the last problem to be solved. I myself have been coming back to it again and again for a dozen years now, and each time I thought there was a clear solution I later discovered that vital things had been left unsaid. At first it seemed to me that Rousseau had already won the argument with Hobbes: had he said that evil is a robust child? Then, as Rousseau argued, children are clumsy, blustering organisms who must take some toll of their environment, who seek activity and self-expansion in an innocent way, but who cannot yet control themselves. Their intentions are not evil, even if their acts cause damage. In this view, man is an energy-converting organism who must exert his manipulative powers, who must damage his world in some ways, who must make it uncomfortable for others, etc., by his own nature as an active being. He seeks self-expansion from a very uncertain power base. Even if man hurts others, it is because he is weak and afraid, not because he is confident and cruel. Rousseau summed up this point of view with the idea that only the strong person can be ethical, not the weak one.

Later I agreed too with the Marxists, that hate and violent aggression could be developed in man as a special kind of cultural orientation, something people learned to do in order to be big and important—as some primitive tribes learned warfare and won social esteem because of their cruelty to enemies, etc. It was not, as Freud had imagined, that man had instincts of hate and aggression, but rather that he could easily be molded in that way by the society which rewarded them. The thing that characterized man was his need for self-esteem, and he would do anything his society wanted in order to earn it.

From this point of view, even scapegoating and the terrible toll it has taken historically seemed to be explainable in Rousseau's terms: the thing that man wanted most was to be part of a close and loving ingroup, to feel at peace and harmony with others of his kind. And to achieve this intimate identification it was necessary to strike at strangers, pull the group together by focusing it on an outside target. So even Hugh Duncan's analysis of the sacrificial ravages of the Nazis could be approached in terms of neutral motives or even altruistic ones: love, harmony, unity. And Hannah Arendt's famous analysis of Eichmann would also fit in with this: here was a simple bureaucrat who wanted only to be admired and rewarded for a job efficiently done and who wielded his rubber stamp on the death of millions with the nonchalance of a postal clerk. We could even, as we have seen, subsume this under the Agape motive: man wants to merge with a larger whole, have something to dedicate his existence to in trustfulness and in humility; he wants to serve the cosmic powers. The most noble human motive, then, would cause the greatest damage because it would lead men to find their highest use as part of an obedient mass, to give their complete devotion and their lives to their leaders. Arthur Koestler, who has one of the best flairs for comprehending the motives of modern men, recently reaffirmed this; in his opinion it is not aggressive drives that have taken the greatest toll in history, but rather "unselfish devotion," "hyper-dependence combined with suggestibility"—the very things discussed in the final pages of the last chapter. In Koestler's view, man is less driven by adrenalin than he is drugged by symbols, by cultural belief systems, by abstractions like flags and anthems: "Wars are fought for words. . . ."[8] Again, Rousseau would be vindicated.

He would also be supported by Erich Fromm's lifelong study of aggression, where he shows that much of it is due to the way children are brought up and the kind of life experiences people have. On this view, the most twisted and vicious people would be those who have been most deprived, most cheated of love, warmth, self-realization. Dr. Strangelove would be the paradigm of the kind of mechanical coldness and life frustration which leads to world destruction.[9] Again, this is a pure Marxist view: changing the life-denying institutions of modern society would enable a new type of human being to take shape.[10] The hope of the Enlightenment in its full development is represented by Fromm: to show *clinically* what prevents self-reliant men. This has been the burden of all of Fromm's work: to argue for the ideal of autonomy while showing precisely what hinders it in the interplay of individual psychology and society. In this way the whole historical problem of slavishness is attacked. People were always ready to yield their wills, to worship the hero, because they were not given a chance for developing initiative, stability, and independence, said the great nineteenth-century Russian sociologist Nikolai Mikhailovsky.[11] Emerson also made this a central teaching of his whole life, holding that man was still a tool of others because he had not developed self-reliance, full and independent insides. Fromm argues that only in this way could man get some kind of even keel, some sort of inner gyroscope that would keep him from alternating eternally between the poles of sadism and masochism.

Contra Rousseau

So much, then, for a sketch of insights into the problem of aggression in human life. As I said, insights like these seemed to me to cover the problem, yet something vital was always left unsaid. It was not until I confronted the work of Rank, and then Brown, that the gap could be filled. Now I think the matter can be pushed to a comprehensive conclusion, that we have a general theory of human evil. Evil is caused by all the things we have outlined, plus the one thing they have left out, the driving impetus that underlies them all: *man's hunger for righteous self-expansion and perpetuation.* No wonder it has taken us so long to pull all the fragmentary insights together, to join the views of both sides on the nature of man. The greatest cause of evil included all human motives in one giant paradox. Good and bad were so inextricably mixed that we couldn't make them out; bad seemed to lead to good, and good motives led to bad. The paradox is that *evil comes from man's urge to heroic victory over evil*. The evil that troubles man most is his vulnerability; he seems impotent to guarantee the absolute meaning of his life, its significance in the cosmos. He assures a plenitude of evil, then, by trying to make closure on his cosmic heroism *in this life and this world*. This is exactly what Rank meant in the epigraph I have used for Chapter Seven: all the intolerable sufferings of mankind result from man's attempt to make the whole world of nature reflect *his* reality, his heroic victory; he thus tries to achieve a perfection on earth, a visible testimonial to his cosmic importance; but this testimonial can only be given conclusively by the beyond, by the source of creation itself which alone knows man's value because it knows his task, the meaning of his life; man has confused two spheres, the visible and whatever is beyond, and this blindness has permitted him to undertake the impossible—to extend the values of his limited visible sphere over all the rest of creation, whatever forms it may take. The tragic evils of history, then, are a commensurate result of a blindness and impossibility of such magnitude.

This explains at the same time the motives that we left unsaid in our sketch. Hobbes was right as well as Rousseau: man is a robustly active creature; activity alone keeps him from going crazy. If he bogs down and begins to dwell on his situation, he risks releasing the neurotic fear repressed into his unconscious—that he is really impotent and will have no effect on the world. So he frantically drives himself to *see* his effects, to convince himself and others that he really counts. This alone is enough to cause evil all by itself: an energetic organism with personal anxieties about his powers. Where is human energy directed if not at objects—human objects most of the time? In other words, man must take out his personal problems on a transference object in one way or another; as psychiatrists now put it, man's whole life is a series of "games" enmeshing himself with others, reflexively and drivenly for the most part, and according to some scenario of power. The playwright Eugene Ionesco summed up what he thought was the real problem of these games in this lament: "As long as we are not assured of immortality, we shall never be fulfilled, we shall go on hating each other in spite of our need for mutual love."[12] The most general statement we could make is that at the very least each person "appropriates" the other in some way so as to perpetuate himself. In this sense, "styles of life" are styles of appropriation of the other to secure one's righteous self-perpetuation. We might say that there is a natural and built-in evil in social life because all interaction is mutual appropriation. We saw a direct example of this in the relation of the leader to the group. Gurus feed on disciples while the disciples are incorporating them; social life seems at times like a science-fiction horror story, with everyone mutually gobbling each other like human spiders.

Historically we saw how this worked in the dialogue between masses and power figures; but we also saw how human energy and fear created evil on the simplest levels of social organization. We talked mostly about spirit-power motives and guilt, but sometimes it was more simple and direct: it could be a matter of sheer physical appetite. Some tribes loved the taste of human flesh and incorporated captive men, women, and children with joy and gusto, with simple stomach motives, we might say—as in Melanesia and among some South American tribes. Sometimes men went to war out of personal frustration in the tribe, to work off sexual jealousy and grief, or even simple boredom.[10] Life on primitive levels could be monotonous, and warfare was often the main source of new experience, travel, real stimulation. In fact, on the primitive level it is almost transparent that warfare was a "game" for appropriating others and enmeshing one's life with them; we see this clearly among the Plains Indians, where warfare was often really a kind of athletic contest between tribes. But organismic urges are by their nature sadistic, and primitive man often wreaked evil on a captured enemy because of his desire to gloat and strut; he tortured to affirm himself, to increase his own sense of importance by humiliating others. And so we see that even without spiritual motives, without otherworldly ambitions of any kind, man causes evil as an organism by enjoying his feeling of animal power. Again, this is what Hobbes saw, that sheer energy causes evil.

My point in lingering on this is to show that we can have no psychology of evil unless we stress the driving personal motives behind man's urge to heroic victory. It may seem on the surface that empty, passive, disinterested people are led like sheep to perform vicious acts, that man easily loses his judgment in the crowd, that he gets carried away by numbers, by shouts, by cleverly phrased slogans and colorful banners—this we might call the "impressionable spectator" theory of aggression.[14] No doubt there is considerable stimulus given to man by the size and enthusiasm of the group around him. After all, he worships power and has to respond to the obvious power of numbers, thrill to the spectacle of masses; it is visible proof that nature favors man if she has made his kind multiply so; she seems on the side of his victory. Another thing, which as Buber saw is that man is stimulated to believe in his heroic destiny by the sight of another human face: it shows the miracle of creation shining out of man, and the fact that this miracle has deep in its eyes and in its head the same beliefs as you, gives you the feeling that your very beliefs are supported by natural creation. Little wonder that the sight and feel of thousands of such miracles moving together with you gives such absolute righteous conviction.

So there is no argument about the fact of mass enthusiasm; the question is how important it is as a cause of aggression. Konrad Lorenz thinks it is perhaps the most important cause,[15] but Freud had already downgraded it in his confrontation of Le Bon and Trotter, the early theorists of "mental contagion" and the "herd mind."[16] Freud asked the question, Why the contagion from the herd? and he found the motive in the person and not in the character of the herd. We know how mobs can be stopped by stopping their leaders, or how panic breaks out when the leader is killed; Freud had explained how the mob identifies with the leader. But beyond that we also saw that man brings his motives in with him when he identifies with power figures. He is suggestible and submissive *because he is waiting* for the magical helper. He gives in to the magic transformation of the group *because he* wants relief of conflict and guilt. He follows the leader's initiatory act because he needs priority magic *so that he can delight* in holy aggression. He moves in to kill the sacrificial scapegoat with the wave of the crowd, not because he is carried along by the wave, but because *he likes* the psychological barter of another life for his own: "You die, not me." The motives and the needs are in men and not in situations or surroundings.* It is true, as Koestler affirms, that man's urge to self-transcendence, his devotion to a cause, has made more butchery than private aggressiveness in history, and that the devastating group hatred is fed by the love of its members, their willingness even to die in its name.[17] We know that as soon as primitives developed identifiable gods and a large social conglomerate to give their loyalty to, their own natural sadistic appetites were translated into the large-scale sacrifices of others that we see in history: one no longer looked for a skull to eat the brains from, or to shrink for magic power, or to plant in the ground facing the enemy so as to mock him—one now couldn't get enough skulls for paving the temple floor, as in Polynesia or West Africa. But Koestler's line of reasoning leads us to a group psychology that would be based only on noble human hopes and not on animal fears—the fact is that the primitive already took the heads of others for his own enhancement, of whatever petty and personal kind. It is true that Eichmann felt physically sick on the one occasion when he actually watched the deadly gas at work, which proves that he was not personally a sadist[18]—but does not prove that he had no personal stake in the killing. As Freud taught us once and for all, men are torn in two by the contradictions that result from their *needs* and not by what they innocently get caught up in. And as Rank added, when they are at their most sheepish and submissive, they are giving vent to the Agape urge in their nature; when they twist and turn to please the leader and the group, they are trying to qualify for absolute goodness and purity so as to be worthy of being included in their transcendence. The individual gives himself to the group because of *his desire* to share in its immortality; we must say, even, that he is willing to die in order *not* to die.

Another way of looking at this is to say that the basic general motive of man—his need for self-esteem, for a feeling of primary value—is not a neutral vessel. True, its contents vary with each

---

* As to the question whether leaders or the group influences these motives more, we would have to study the matter along the lines that Redl developed: it would probably depend on whether the heroic cause had a definite form and continuity which would be felt by the members independently of a particular leader (say, the Allied cause in World War II) or whether the leader himself gave form and continuity to the cause, embodied it and represented it in his own person (as did Hitler and Napoleon).

individual and with each society; people learn different ways of feeling warm self-value. I myself have written and argued that the self-esteem motive is elastic and neutral, but I now see that this is not quite so. True, there are no instincts that absolutely determine when people should feel good about themselves. But self-esteem is equivalent to "righteousness" or feeling "right." Which means that self-esteem is based on an active passion: man cannot feel right unless he lives the heroic victory over evil, the assurance of immortality. From the beginning, then, the self-esteem is loaded with this task universally, and given its form by how it resolves this task. Which, of course, is another way of saying that the self-esteem is based on the cultural continuation of the *causa sui* project in the child. This is how it has always been understood, only now we add that the character of this *causa sui* project is definite and inflexible: the securing of immortality (in whichever way this is understood by the individual and the society).

Along with this we have to make an important addition to Fromm's approach to aggression. It is true that frustrated, deprived, weak, unindividuated people commit aggression very readily; clinical records are eloquent on this. It is true too that there are mechanical people who fear life, who need to control things with a secure sense of power, who prefer inanimate objects to living ones, etc. Fromm calls them "necrophiles," or lovers of death, in opposition to "biophiles," or lovers of life. This is a valuable distinction in character structures because it helps us to focus on different ways of bringing up children which might lead to one or the other general orientation—to a love of life which develops sentiments of warm humanity or to a "syndrome of decay" which stifles these sentiments. If we could, we would certainly want to avoid raising generations of young who respect computers more than they do others. Fromm says that one explanation of the fact that the world is now bordering on nuclear destruction is the widespread prevalence of a modern *Homo mechanicus*. It may be, he says, that people do not fear total destruction because they do not love life, or are indifferent to it, or even are attracted to death, fascinated by the prospect of total destruction.[19]

From all we know, I think it would be nearer the truth to talk about a cultural type of man who earns his immortality from identification with the powers of machines, rather than a simple lover of death. Mass destruction committed under the reign of God the Machine is a tribute to the expansion of an implacable, efficient force with which modern men can identify—it would not be an attraction to the stillness of death itself. This attraction seems to me more of a Buddhistic sentiment—that is, the achievement of a certain kind of maturity and transcendence. The mechanical man may scorn and fear living things, but I think it is precisely because he feels that they do not have the power over life and death that machines have; his eternity symbol is then the machine which transcends both life and death. Even for a Hitler death was not an end in itself, but a power transformation to a higher vitality, a better order.

But all this is simply a minor dilemma of clarification of cultural and clinical types; it will take very much more work to sort these things out, and we may never be able to do it in any but a very gross and suggestive way. There is something much more crucial at stake in Fromm's attempt to place the problem of aggression on a continuum from normal types to pathological ones. And we right away know what it is: not only weak, or mechanical, or pathological, or "primitive and elemental" types aggress, but also fat, jolly ones—people who have had abundant childhood care and love! The man who dropped the atomic bomb is the warm, gentle boy who grew up next door. The kings of Dahomey who signaled annually for the heads of hundreds of murdered prisoners to be piled in heaps very likely had a child-rearing experience that Margaret Mead could have written about favorably. The reason is positive and simple: man aggresses not only out of frustration and fear but out of joy, plenitude, love of life. *Men kill lavishly out of the sublime joy of heroic triumph over evil. Voilà tout.* What are clinical classifications and niceties going to do with that?

It is true, I think, that a weak man will more easily, if pushed, buy off his own death by taking another, and that a strong man will be less likely to do this. It is true, too, that most men will not usually kill unless it is under the banner of some kind of fight against evil; in which case one is tempted, like Koestler, to blame the banner, the propaganda and artificial belief system, and not the men. But banners don't wrap themselves around men: men invent banners and clutch at them; they hunger for believable words that dress life in convincing meaning. As Dostoevsky so well put it, men would die if they didn't have nice words to speak (to make sense out of their occasions). They would die, not because words are nice trimmings to life, but because without words action stops dead, and when action stops the gnawing realization of impotency and the dumb futility of animal life begins. Words abolish fear and embody hope in themselves. I think it is time for social scientists to catch up with Hitler as a psychologist, and to realize that men will do anything for heroic belonging to a victorious cause if they are persuaded about the legitimacy of that cause. And I know no psychology, and so far no conditions on this earth, which would exempt man from fulfilling his urge to cosmic heroism, which means from identifying evil and moving against it. In all cases but one this means moving also against individuals who embody evil. The one case, of course, is the teaching of the great religions, and in its modern guise pacifism, or nonviolence. This is a 2,000-year-old ideal at which descriptive psychology stops, since it is an ideal that has hardly yet made a dent in the affairs and minds of men. But we will return to this vital matter of values in the conclusion of this book.

[It was at this stage in the original manuscript that the decision was made to cut material devoted to a study of the modern approaches to Darwinism, which now appears as a unique publication elsewhere.* In essence the author's intention in the eliminated pages was to help bridge the gap between the biological and cultural scientists on the issue of human motives. Differences between the two camps of scientists are seen as differences in premises and approaches and not in the conclusions drawn. There is agreement among scientists on man's basic animality—the fact that he is conditioned by the environment, that he does not act freely, altogether rationally, or with full self-knowledge.

Lorenz, Darwin, Freud, Rank, and Brown all see irrationality as a fundamental part of man. The author's plea is for taking a larger

---

* The interested reader is directed to "Toward the Merger of Animal and Human Studies," *Philosophy of the Social Sciences*, vol. 4, nos. 2–3, June–September 1974, pp. 235–254.

*phenomenological field approach and viewing man as an animal
who enjoys organismic self-expansion, needs to feel powerful and
to banish death. With this approach both the basic animality and
the larger phenomenological problems missed by instinctual re-
ductionism are dealt with.*]

Conclusion: The Shape of Social Theory

As we saw earlier, inequality did not arise as the radicals thought
—only with the advent of private property and the growth of
state structures of domination. Nor was it as "natural" as the conservatives wanted: oppressive power has always been in the service
of "the legitimate order."[20] Similarly, human nature is not as neutral
as Rousseau and Marx wanted; nor is it as ineluctably evil as conservatives like to make out in order to keep the status quo. Radical
theorists must realize that if you give men political and economic
equality, they will still welcome unfreedom in some form. Conservatives must know that the freedom to obey or not to obey, to delegate
one's powers to authority, is not so free: it is coerced in the very
beginning and by the very nature of man's perceptions of power and
majesty. The "talents" that men use to amass wealth and social
privilege may be due to some real differences in quality of mind
and body; but the talent to mystify others is the queen of tyranny,
and it is not all natural and neutral, but partly man-made—made
by ignorance, thirst for illusion, and fear. As such, it is part of the
scientific problem of human liberation, and is not destined to
remain wholly in the natural order of things.[21]

If the complexities of the psychological dimensions of inequality
and the unfreedom at the heart of human nature are sure to please
no one who is firmly embedded in an ideological camp, then it
becomes even more difficult to know what we are going to do about
them or how we are going to approach them. The pluralism of
ideologies will continue to talk and act past them. But a few things
seem clear: although the radicals may not like it, the science of
society will have to go much more slowly and modestly than was at
first realized by Rousseau and Marx. Unless, of course, it subserves

violent revolution—in which case, as we have learned to our sorrow, the new society that comes into being has even less chance of being openly scientific. As for the conservatives, although they may shrink back in fear, there is nothing to prevent the science of man from being the absolutely critical and meliorative science of society that was envisioned in the Enlightenment. There is nothing in human nature that dooms in advance the most thoroughgoing social changes and utopian ambitions. It used to be thought, for example, that if man's innate aggressiveness was a drive that had to find expression, then all societies had to have some means of "hate satisfaction." No less an anthropologist than Clyde Kluckhohn maintained that.[22] Many of our best minds have been tortuously struggling with the implications of this: it did not seem possible to have any kind of humanistic, liberating social theory if man carried within himself the seeds of destructiveness.[23] And certainly the facts of the history of war and scapegoating seem to have borne out Kluckhohn and Freud and hosts of others. But if hate is not a basic drive or a quantum of instinct, but instead results from the fear of death and impotency and can be relieved by a heroic victory over a hate object, then at least we have some scientific purchase on the problem. A science of man in society is possible even while admitting the most destructive motives of men, precisely because these motives become open and amenable to clear analysis, to a tracing out of their total structure in the full field of human affairs as those affairs reflect the torments of man's inner life, his existential paradoxes.

Social theory, then, is neither radical nor conservative, but scientific; and we should begin to get scientific agreement on its basic image of man and society. If we have an agreed image in a science, there is nothing to prevent us from moving on to the kinds of social designs that we talked about in Chapter Eight: designs for the possibility of nondestructive yet victorious types of social systems. We have a general theory of human nature that is entirely "naturalistic," as Kenneth Burke wanted, and one that could theoretically "immunize mankind" to its "natural weakness"—the scapegoating for its own fears and needs. A social ideal could be designed that takes into account man's basest motives, but now an ideal not directly negated by those motives. In others words, a hate object need not be any special class or race or even human enemy, but could be things that take impersonal but real forms, like poverty, disease, oppression, natural disasters, etc. Or, if we know that evil takes human form in oppressors and hangmen, then we could at least try to make our hatreds of men intelligent and informed: we could work against the enemies of freedom, those who thrive on slavery, on the gullibilities and weaknesses of their fellow man, as Burke so eloquently argued.[24]

I admit in concluding that this raises more problems than it solves, since men hate and love according to their individual understandings and personal needs. But we have to try to take things one step further; the whole thrust of the science of man since the Enlightenment has been after all a promise that objectivity about evil is possible. This objectivity about evil introduces what we might call the possibility of objective hatred. This clarification of hatred would allow us, once more, to make the circle on James's timeless plea for a moral equivalent to natural sadism, to hope to translate our self-expansion into a furtherance of life instead of the destruction of it. Finally, if we know that we ourselves hate because of the same needs and urges to heroic victory over evil as those we hate, there is perhaps no better way to begin to introduce milder justice into the affairs of men. This is the great moral that Albert Camus drew from our demonic times, when he expressed the moving hope that a day would come when each person would proclaim in his own fashion the superiority of being wrong without killing others than being right in the quiet of the charnel house.

Retrospect and Conclusion:
What Is the Heroic Society?

> . . . if we can no longer live the great symbolisms
> of the sacred in accordance with the original belief
> in them, we can, we modern men, aim at a second
> naiveté in and through criticism.
> Paul Ricoeur[1]

I have come a long way and laid a lot of ink on the pulp of dead trees; it is now time to justify this expenditure of nature's bounty, not to mention the reader's indulgence. The only way to do this would be to show that what we know about man tells us about the *possibilities* for man, even though we have sketched a rather pathetic portrait of him. If we have really gotten at what makes people act the way they do, at basic human motives, then we can really talk intelligently to the question that is the most intimate to our heart—what men have always yearned to know, namely, What is possible?

As far as the science of man is concerned, many thinkers since the Enlightenment have believed that everything is possible for a science of society. Rousseau, Marx, Owens—the whole school of utopian socialists and still today modern revolutionaries in all continents believe this. All we have to do, they claim, is to change the structure of things and a new society will emerge like a splendid phoenix free of all impurity and evil, because evil lies not in the hearts of men but in the social arrangements that men take for granted. Men forget, wrote the medieval Arab historian Ibn Khaldun, how things were in the beginning, free and equal under tribalism; they grow up under the new system of kingship and the state and so they imagine that things were always this way and they accept them without complaint. Marx repeated the identical thesis centuries later: men live abased under tyranny and self-delusion because they no longer understand the conditions of natural freedom. Revolutionaries still today trumpet this philosophy of history as the fall of pure men into corrupt social structures.

The reason the philosophy is so attractive is that men need hopes and ideals to urge them on—they need possibility, belief in themselves in order to even try to make things better. All truths are part-truths as far as creatures are concerned, and so there is nothing wrong with an illusion that is creative. Up to a point, of course: the point at which the illusion lies about something very important, such as human nature. If it is false to that, then it becomes oppressive, because if you try falsely to make a new beginning you fail. I know that this bit of wisdom is already stale to our epoch, but even in its staleness we can't let go of it. We still live in its shadow: the state tyranny of Soviet Russia is the steady, daily, empirical reminder of the costs of ignoring the psychology of man. Marxism in its traditional form is simply not a correct guide for a new society. But the irony is that we simply do not know what to do with this stale truth. That is why there is such a crisis in Marxist thought, in leftist-humanist thought. What is a truly mature, sophisticated Marxism? And if we put such a thing together, where does it point on the problems of society? Does the union of Marx and Freud eclipse the Enlightenment vision for a science of society? If not, what kind of science can we imagine and work toward? These are the vital, aching questions of the contemporary scientific conscience; what kind of answers does our present knowledge suggest?

History

Well, for one thing—one great thing—we now see history as it really has been in terms of overall psychodynamics. From the outside a saga of tyranny, violence, coercion; from the inside, self-delusion and self-enslavement. From earliest times men asked to be mystified, and right away there were those ready to fill the role.

Men put on the chains imposed by the powers of dead ancestors, then shamans, priests, divine kings, heads of state. Today we understand the inner dynamics of this long history of self-abasement: men *need* transference in order to be able to stand life. Man immunizes himself against terror by controlling his fascination, by localizing it and developing working responses toward the sources of it. The result is that he becomes a reflex of small terrors and small fascinations in place of overwhelming ones. It is a forced and necessary barter: the exchange of unfreedom for life. From this point of view history is the career of a frightened animal who has to deaden himself against life in order to live. And it is this very deadening that takes such a toll of others' lives.

All organisms want to perpetuate themselves, continue to experience and to live. It is a great mystery that we don't understand but observe every day: we are amazed, as we try to club a cornered rat, how frantically he wants to live. All animals are this frantic, without even knowing what death means; they probably only sense the danger of crushing opposing power; this is as far as the "instinct of self-preservation" takes them, out of the way of what threatens to overwhelm and engulf them. For all organisms, then, opposing and obliterating power is evil—it threatens to stop experience. But men are truly sorry creatures because they have made death conscious. They can see evil in anything that wounds them, causes ill health, or even deprives them of pleasure. Consciousness means too that they have to be preoccupied with evil even in the absence of any immediate danger; their lives become a meditation on evil and a planned venture for controlling it and forestalling it.

The result is one of the great tragedies of human existence, what we might call the need to "fetishize evil," to locate the threat to life in some special places where it can be placated and controlled. It is tragic precisely because it is sometimes very arbitrary: men make fantasies about evil, see it in the wrong places, and destroy themselves and others by uselessly thrashing about. This is the great moral of Melville's *Moby Dick*, the specific tragedy of a man driven to confine all evil to the person of a white whale.[2] The result is that he pulls down around his shoulders the lives of almost all those he comes in contact with.

A second result of man's animal vulnerability to death and his symbolic consciousness of it is the struggle to get power to fortify himself. Other animals must simply use those powers that nature provided them with and the neural circuits that animate those powers. But man can invent and imagine powers, and he can invent ways to protect power. This means, as Nietzsche saw and shocked his world with, that all moral categories are power categories; they are not about virtue in any abstract sense. Purity, goodness, rightness—these are ways of keeping power intact so as to cheat death; the striving for perfection is a way of qualifying for extraspecial immunity not only in this world but in others to come. Hence all categories of dirt, filth, imperfection, and error are *vulnerability* categories, power problems. For young children *Band-Aids* are already an obsessive religion that sets the whole tone of it: cleanliness is safety.

So we see that as an organism man is fated to perpetuate himself and as a conscious organism he is fated to identify evil as the threat to that perpetuation. In the same way, he is driven to individuate himself as an organism, to develop his own peculiar talents and personality. And what, then, would be the highest development and use of those talents? To contribute to the struggle against evil, of course. In other words, man is fated, as William James saw, to consider this earth as a theater for heroism, and his life as a vehicle for heroic acts which aim precisely to transcend evil. Each person wants to have his life make a difference in the life of mankind, contribute in some way toward securing and furthering that life, make it in some ways less vulnerable, more durable. To be a true hero is to triumph over disease, want, death. One knows that his life has had vital human meaning if it has been able to bring real benefits to the life of mankind. And so men have always honored their heroes, especially in religion, medicine, science, diplomacy, and war. Here is where heroism has been most easily identifiable. From Constantine and Christ to Churchill and De Gaulle, men have called their heroes "saviors" in the literal sense: those who have delivered them from the evil of the termination of life, either of their own immediate lives or of the duration of their people. Even more, by his own death the hero secures the lives of others, and so the greatest heroic sacrifice, as Frazer taught us, is the sacrifice of the god for his people. We see this in Oedipus at Colonus, in Christ, and today in the embalmed Lenin. The giants died to secure mankind; by their blood we are saved. It is almost pathetically logical how man the supremely vulnerable animal developed the cult of the heroic.

But if we add together the logic of the heroic with the necessary fetishization of evil, we get a formula that is no longer pathetic but terrifying. It explains almost all by itself why man, of all animals, has caused the most devastation on earth—the most real evil. He struggles extra hard to be immune to death because he alone is conscious of it; but by being able to identify and isolate evil arbitrarily, he is capable of lashing out in all directions against imagined dangers of this world. This means that in order to live he is capable of bringing a large part of the world down around his shoulders. History is just such a testimonial to the frightening costs of heroism. The hero is the one who can go out and get added powers by killing an enemy and taking his talismans or his scalp or eating his heart. He becomes a walking repository of accrued powers. Animals can only take in food for power; man can literally take in the trinkets and bodies of his whole world. Furthermore, the hero proves his power by winning in battle; he shows that he is favored by the gods. Also, he can appease the gods by offering to them the sacrifice of the stranger. The hero is, then, the one who accrues power by his acts, and who placates invisible powers by his expiations. He kills those who threaten his group, he incorporates their powers to further protect his group, he sacrifices others to gain immunity for his group. In a word, he becomes a savior through blood. From the head-hunting and charm-hunting of the primitives to the holocausts of Hitler, the dynamic is the same: the heroic victory over evil by a traffic in pure power. And the aim is the same: purity, goodness, righteousness—immunity. Hitler Youth were recruited on the basis of idealism; the nice boy next door is the one who dropped the bomb on Hiroshima; the idealistic communist is the one who sided with Stalin against his former comrades: kill to protect the heroic revolution, to assure the victory over evil. As Dostoevsky saw, killing is sometimes distasteful, but the distaste is swallowed if it is necessary to true heroism: as one of the revolutionaries asked Pyotr Verhovensky in *The Possessed*, when they were about to kill one of their number, "Are other groups also doing this?" In other words, is it the socially heroic thing to do, or are we being arbitrary about identifying evil? Each person wants his life to be a marker for good as his group defines it. Men work their programs of heroism according to the standard cultural scenarios, from Pontius Pilate through Eichmann and Calley. It is as Hegel long ago said: men cause evil out of good intentions, not out of wicked ones. Men cause evil by wanting heroically to triumph over it, because man is a frightened animal who tries to triumph, an animal who will not admit his own insignificance, that he cannot perpetuate himself and his group forever, that no one is invulnerable no matter how much of the blood of others is spilled to try to demonstrate it.

Another way of summing up this whole matter is to contrast Hegel's view of evil out of good intentions with Freud's view, which was very specifically focused on evil *motives*. Freud saw evil as a fatality for man, forever locked in the human breast. This is what gave Freud such a dim view of the future of man. Many eyes looked to a man of his greatness for a prophecy on human possibilities, but he refused to pose as the magician-seer and give men the false comfort of prediction. As he put it in a late writing:

I have not the courage to rise up before my fellow-men as a prophet, and I bow to their reproach that I can offer them no consolation. . . .[3]

This is a heavy confession by one of history's greatest students of men; but I am citing it not for its honesty or humility, but because of the reason for its pathos. The future of man was problematic for Freud because of the instincts that have driven man and will supposedly always drive him. As he put it, right after the above admission and at the very end of his book:

The fateful question for the human species seems to me to be whether and to what extent [it] . . . will succeed in mastering . . . the human instinct of aggression and self-destruction.

The most that men can seem to do is to put a veneer of civilization and reason over this instinct; but the problem of evil is "born afresh with every child," as Freud wrote three years earlier, in 1927, and it takes the form of precise instinctual wishes—incest, lust for killing, cannibalism.[4] This was man's repugnant heritage, a heritage that he seems forever destined to work upon the world. Kant's famous observation on man was now not merely a philosophical aphorism but a scientific judgment: "From the crooked wood of which man is made, nothing quite straight can be built."

Yet today we know that Freud was wrong about evil. Man is a crooked wood all right, but not in the way that Freud thought. This is a crucial difference because it means that we do not have to follow Freud on the exact grounds of his feelings for the problematic of the human future. If, instead, we follow Rank and the general science of man, we get a quite different picture of the oldest "instinctual wishes." Incest is an immortality motive, it symbolizes the idea of self-fertilization, as Jung has so well written[5]—the defeat of biology and the fatality of species propagation. For the child in the family it may be an identity motive, a way of immediately becoming an individual and stepping out of the collective role of obedient child by breaking up the family ideology, as Rank so brilliantly argued.[6] Historically, the brother-sister marriage of ancient kings like the Pharaohs must have been a way of preserving and increasing the precious mana power that the king possessed. Cannibalism, it is true, has often been motivated by sheer appetite for meat, the pleasures of incorporation of a purely sensual kind, quite free of any spiritual overtones. But as just noted, much of the time the motive is one of mana power. Which largely explains why cannibalism becomes uniformly repugnant to men when the spirit-power beliefs that sustained it are left behind; if it were a matter of instinctual appetite, it would be more tenacious. And as for the lust for killing, this too, we now know, is largely a psychological problem; it is not primarily a matter of the satisfaction of vicious animal aggression. We know that men often kill with appetite and excitement, as well as real dedication, but this is only logical for animals who are born hunters and who enjoy the feeling of maximizing their organismic powers at the expense of a trapped and helpless prey.

This much evolution and some million years of prehistory may have given us; but to talk about satisfying one's appetites for purity and heroism with a certain relish and style is not to say that this relish is itself the motive for the appetite. Freud thought it was man's appetite that undid him, but actually it is his animal limitation as we now understand it. The tragedy of evolution is that it created a limited animal with unlimited horizons. Man is the only animal that is not armed with the natural instinctive mechanisms or programming for shrinking his world down to a size that he can automatically act on. This means that men have to artificially and arbitrarily restrict their intake of experience and focus their output of decisive action. Men have to keep from going mad by biting off small pieces of reality which they can get some command over and some organismic satisfaction from. This means that their noblest passions are played out in the most narrow and unreflective ways, and this is what undoes them. From this point of view the main problematic for the future of man has to be expressed in the following paradox: Man is an animal who must fetishize in order to survive and to have "normal mental health." But this shrinkage of vision that permits him to survive also at the same time prevents him from having the overall understanding he needs to plan for and control the effects of his shrinkage of experience. A paradox this bitter sends a chill through all reflective men. If Freud's famous "fateful question for the human species" was not exactly the right one, the paradox is no less fateful. It seems that the experiment of man may well prove to be an evolutionary dead end, an impossible animal—one who, individually, needs for healthy action the very conduct that, on a general level, is destructive to him. It is maddeningly perverse. And even if we bring Freud's views on evil into line with Hegel's, there is no way of denying that Freud's pessimism about the future is just as securely based. as if man did actually have evil *motives*.

But it does influence the whole perspective on history which I am sketching here. History and its incredible tragedy and drivenness then become a record of understandable folly. It is the career of a frightened animal who must lie in order to live—or, better, in order to live the distinctive style that his nature fits him for. The thing that feeds the great destructiveness of history is that men give their entire allegiance to their own group; and each group is a codified hero system. Which is another way of saying that societies are standardized systems of death denial; they give structure to the formulas for heroic transcendence. History can then be looked at as a succession of immortality ideologies, or as a mixture at any time of several of these ideologies. We can ask about any epoch, What are the social forms of heroism available? And we can take a sweep over history and see how these forms vary and how they animate each epoch. For primitive man, who practiced the ritual renewal of nature, each person could be a cosmic hero of a quite definite kind: he could contribute with his powers and observances to the replenishment of cosmic life. Gradually, as societies became more complex and differentiated into classes, cosmic heroism became the property of special classes like divine kings and the military, who were charged with the renewal of nature and the protection of the group by means of their own special powers. And so the situation developed where men could be heroic only by following orders. Men had given the mandate of power and expiation to their leader-heroes, and so salvation had to be mediated to them by these figures. In a primitive hunting band or a tribe the leader cannot compel anyone to go to war; in the kingship and the state the subjects have no choice. They now serve in warfare heroism *for* the divine king who provides his own power in victory and bathes the survivors in it. With the rise of money coinage one could be a money hero and privately protect himself and his offspring by the accumulation of visible gold-power. With Christianity something new came into the world: the heroism of renunciation of this world and the satisfactions of this life, which is why the pagans thought Christianity was crazy. It was a sort of antiheroism by an animal who denied life in order to deny evil. Buddhism did the same thing even more extremely, denying all possible worlds. In modern times, with the Enlightenment, began again a new paganism of the exploitation and enjoyment of earthly life, partly as a reaction against the Christian renunciation of the world. Now a new type of productive and scientific hero came into prominence, and we are still living this today. More cars produced by Detroit, higher stock-market prices, more profits, more goods moving—all this equals more heroism. And with the French Revolution another type of modern hero was codified: the revolutionary hero who will bring an end to injustice and evil once and for all, by bringing into being a new utopian society perfect in its purity.

Psychology

This is hardly a complete catalogue of culturally codified heroics, but it is a good representation of the ideologies that have taken such a toll of life; in each of the above examples masses of human lives have been piled up in order for the cultural transcendence to be achieved. And there is nothing "perverse" about it because it represents the expression of the fullest expansive life of the heroic animal. We can talk for a century about what causes human aggression; we can try to find the springs in animal instincts, or we can try to find them in bottled-up hatreds due to frustration or in some kind of miscarried experiences of early years, of poor child handling and training. All these would be true, but still trivial because men kill out of joy, in the experience of expansive transcendence over evil. This poses an immense problem for social theory, a problem that we have utterly failed to be clear about. If men kill out of heroic joy, in what direction do we program for improvements in human nature? What are we going to improve if men work evil out of the impulse to righteousness and goodness? What kind of child-rearing programs are we going to promote—with Fromm, Horney, et al.—in order to bring in the humanistic millenium, if men are aggressive in order to expand life, if aggression in the service of life is man's highest creative act? If we were to be logical, these childhood programs would have to be something that eliminates joy and heroic self-expansion in order to be effective for peace. And how could we ever get controlled child-rearing programs without the most oppressive social regulation?

The cataloguing of maddening dilemmas such as these are, for utopian thought, could probably be continued to fill a whole book; let me add merely a few more. We know that to be human is to be neurotic in some ways and to some degree; there is no way to become an adult without serious twisting of one's perceptions of the world. Even more, it is not the especially twisted people who are most dangerous: coprophiliacs are harmless, rapists do not do the damage to life that idealistic leaders do. Also, leaders are a function of the "normal" urges of masses to some large extent; this means that even psychically crippled leaders are an expression of the widespread urge to heroic transcendence. Dr. Strangelove was surely a psychic cripple, but he was not an evil genius who moved everyone around him to his will; he was simply one clever computer in a vast idealistic program to guarantee the survival of the "free world." Today we are living the grotesque spectacle of the poisoning of the earth by the nineteenth-century hero system of unrestrained material production. This is perhaps the greatest and most pervasive evil to have emerged in all of history, and it may even eventually defeat all of mankind. Still there are no "twisted" people whom we can hold responsible for this.

I know all this is more or less obvious, but it puts our discussion on the proper plane; it teaches us one great lesson—a pill that for modern man may be the bitterest of all to swallow—namely, that we seem to be unable to approach the problem of human evil from the side of psychology. Freud, who gave us the ideal of the psychological liberation of man, also gave us many glimpses of its limitations. I am not referring here to his cynicism about what men may accomplish because of the perversity of their natures, but rather to his admission that there is no dependable line between normal and abnormal in affairs of the human world. In the most characteristic human activity—love—we see the most distortion of reality. Talking about the distortions of transference-love, Freud says:

. . . it is to a high degree lacking in regard for reality, is less sensible, less concerned about consequences, more blind in its estimation of the person loved, than we are willing to admit of normal love.

And then he is forced to take most of this back, honest thinker that he is, by concluding that:

We should not forget, however, that it is precisely these departures from the norm that make up the essential element in the condition of being in love.[7]

In other words, transference is the only ideality that man has. It was no news to Freud that the ability to love and to believe is a matter of susceptibility to illusion. He prided himself on being a stoical scientist who had transcended the props of illusion, yet he retained his faith in science—in psychoanalysis—as his particular hero system. This is the same as saying that all hero systems are based on illusion except one's own, which is somehow in a special, privileged place, as if given in nature herself. Rank got right at the heart of Freud's dilemma:

Just as he himself could so easily confess his agnosticism while he had created for himself a private religion, it seems that, even in his intellectual and rational achievements, he still had to express and assert his irrational needs by at least fighting for and about his rational ideas.[8]

This is perfect. It means that Freud, too, was not exempt from the need to fit himself into a scheme of cosmic heroism, an immortality ideology that had to be taken on faith. This is why Rank saw the need to go "beyond psychology": it cannot by itself substitute for a hero system unless it is—as it was for Freud—*the* hero system that guaranteed him immortality. This is the meaning of Rank's critique of psychology as "self-deception." It cannot contain the immortality urge characteristic of life. It is just another ideology "which is gradually trying to supplant religious and moral ideology," but "is only partially qualified to do this, because it is a preponderantly negative and disintegrating ideology."[9] In other words, all that psychology has really accomplished is to make the inner life the subject matter of science, and in doing this it dissipated the idea of the soul. But it was the soul which once linked man's inner life to a transcendent scheme of cosmic heroism. Now the individual is stuck with himself and with an inner life that he can only analyze away as a product of social conditioning. Psychological introspection took cosmic heroics and made them self-reflective and isolated. At best it gives the person a new self-acceptance—but this is not what man wants or needs: one cannot generate a self-created hero system unless he is mad. Only pure narcissistic megalomania can banish guilt.

It was on the point of guilt, as Rank saw, that Freud's system of heroism fell down. He admonishes Freud with the didactic mocking of one who possesses a clearly superior conceptualization:

It is with his therapeutic attempt to remove the guilt by tracing it back "causally" to the individual's experience in childhood that Freud steps in. How presumptuous, and at the same time, naive, is this idea of simply removing human guilt by explaining it causally as "neurotic"![10]

Exactly. Guilt is a reflection of the problem of acting in the universe; only partly is it connected to the accidents of one's birth and early experience. Guilt, as the existentialists put it, is the guilt of *being* itself. It reflects the self-conscious animal's bafflement at having emerged from nature, at sticking out too much without knowing what for, at not being able to securely place himself in an eternal meaning system. How presumptuous of psychology to claim to be able to handle a problem of these dimensions. As Progoff has so brilliantly summed up psychology after Freud, it all culminates once again in a recognition of the magnitude of the problem of cosmic heroism.[11]

This is what Adler meant when he summed up in a simplified way a basic insight of his whole life's work, "All neurosis is vanity."[12] Neurosis, in other words, reflects the incapacity of the individual to heroically transcend himself; when he tries in one way or another, it is plainly vain. We are back again to a famous fruit of Rank's work too, his insight that neurosis "is at bottom always only incapacity for illusion."[13] But we are back to it with a vengeance and with the broadest possible contemporary understanding. Transference represents not only the necessary and inevitable, but the *most creative* distortion of reality. As Buber said, reality for man is something he must imagine, search out in the eyes of his fellows, with their gleam of passionate dedication. This is also what Jung intimates about the vitality of transference when he calls it "kinship libido."[14] This means that men join together their individual pulsations in a gamble toward something transcendent. Life imagines its own significance and strains to justify its beliefs. It is as though the life force itself needed illusion in order to further itself.

Logically, then, the ideal creativity for man would strain toward the grandest illusion.

The Science of Man

Well, obviously, none of this has been unimpeachable to the critics over the years. Words like "irrationality," "illusion," "wilful and heroic dedication"—these rub many people the wrong way. They have hardly helped make our world any better, especially in modern times. Erich Fromm, for example, impugned Rank's whole system of thought by arguing how perfectly suited it was as a philosophy for fascists.[15] The essay in which this was done was not an essay to bring any credit to Fromm as a thinker; but it was animated in part at least by the demonic crisis of the times, by Hitlerism, and in spite of its shabbiness it did convey a truth, the need to be wary of life-enhancing illusions.

It is precisely at this point that the science of man comes in. We know that Nazism was a viable hero system that lived the illusion of the defeat of evil on earth. We know the terrifying dynamic of victimage and scapegoating all across history, and we know what it means—the offering of the other's body in order to buy off one's own death, the sadistic formula *par excellence:* break the bones and spill the blood of the victim in the service of some "higher truth" that the sacrificers alone possess. To treat the body with the same scorn that God seems to treat it is to draw closer to Him. Well, we know these things only too well in our time. The problem is what to do with them. Men cannot abandon the heroic. If we say that the irrational or mythical is part of human groping for transcendence, we do not give it any blanket approval. But groups of men can do what they have always done—argue about heroism, assess the costs of it, show that it is self-defeating, a fantasy, a dangerous illusion and not one that is life-enhancing and ennobling.[16] As Paul Pruyser so well put it, "The great question is: If illusions are needed, how can we have those that are capable of correction, and how can we have those that will not deteriorate into delusions?"[17] If men live in myths and not absolutes, there is nothing we can do or say about that. But we can argue for nondestructive myths; this is the task of what would be a general science of society.*

I have argued elsewhere that one very graphic way of looking at mental illness is to see it as the laying onto others of one's own hyperfears of life and death. From this perspective we can also see that leaders of nations, citizens of so-called democracies, "normal men" are also doing the very same thing all the time: laying their power-expiation immunity trip onto everyone else. Today the whole world is already becoming uncomfortable with the repeated "war games" and hydrogen-bomb tests by nations on power trips, tests that lay their danger onto innocent and powerless neighbors. In a way it is the drama of the family and the Feifferian love affair writ large across the face of the planet, the "family" of nations. There are no particular leaders or special councils of elite to blame in all this, simply because most people identify with the symbols of power and agree to them. The nation offers immortality to all its members. Again, Erich Fromm was wrong to argue that psychically crippled people, what he calls "necrophilic characters," do evil things by valuing death over life and so lay waste to life because it makes them uncomfortable. Life makes whole nations of normal people uncomfortable, and hence the serene accord and abandon with which men have defeated themselves all through history.

This is the great weakness, as we have now discovered, of Enlightenment rationalism, the easy hope that by the spread of reason men will stand up to their full size and renounce irrationality. The Enlightenment thinkers understood well the dangers of the mass mind, and they thought that by the spread of science and education all this could change. The great Russian sociologist Nikolai Mikhailovsky had already singled out the hero as the enemy of democracy, the one who causes others to yield their wills because of the safety he offers them.[18] The thing that had to be done was to prevent society from turning the individual into a tool for the sake

---

* This admission of the need for guiding heroic myths, and at the same time the plea to be wary of their costs, reconciles a long-standing argument in social theory: the challenge that Georges Sorel threw down in his critique of reason as a guide in social life. Social scientists had to admit that Sorel had something, yet at the same time they could not admit it, since it seemed to leave them no role as the representatives of reason.

of social efficiency and safety. How could the infringement of individuality be overcome? Mikhailovsky answered in the same vein as modern humanist psychiatrists: by giving the individual the opportunity for harmonious development.[19] At about the same time that other great Enlightenment man, Emerson, made his famous plea for self-reliance, for persons with full and independent insides so that they could have the stability to withstand herd enthusiasms and herd fears.

This whole tradition was brought up to date by Herbert Marcuse in a brilliant essay on the ideology of death. He argued that death has always been used by leaders and elites as an ideology to get the masses to conform and to yield up their autonomy. Leaders win allegiance to the cultural *causa sui* project because it protects against vulnerability. The polis, the state, god—all these are symbols of infallibility in which the masses willingly embed their fearful freedoms.[20] There we have it: the culmination of the Enlightenment in a proper focus on the fundamental dynamics of mass slavishness. On the highest level of sophistication we know in detail what men fear and how they deny that fear. There is a single line from Emerson through Mikhailovsky up to Fromm and Marcuse.

But wait. We said that Enlightenment rationalism was too easy a creed, and so we would expect to see this weakness in all its thinkers, and Marcuse is no exception when he naively says:

. . . death [is] the ultimate cause of all anxiety, [and] sustains unfreedom. Man is not free as long as death has not become really "his own," that is, as long as it has not been brought under his autonomy.[21]

Alas, the fact is that men do not have any autonomy under which to bring things. This great and fundamental problem for the whole career of Enlightenment science was posed by Rank:

Whether the individual is at all in a position to grow beyond . . . [some kind of transference justification, some form of moral dependence] and to affirm and accept himself *from himself* cannot be said. Only in the creative type does this seem possible *to some extent*. . . .[22]

But it can be said, and Rank says it: even the highest, most individuated creative type can only manage autonomy to some extent.

The fact is that men cannot and do not stand on their own powers; therefore they cannot make death "their own." Moral dependence—guilt—is a natural motive of the human condition and has to be absolved from something beyond oneself. One young revolutionary once admonished me in saying that "guilt is not a motive"; he never saw that *his* guilt was absorbed by submission to the revolutionary cell. The weakness of the Enlightenment, then, was that it did not understand human nature—and it apparently still does not. Marcuse, in an eloquent line, asks for "the good conscience to be a coward," the uprooting of heroic sublimation.[23] But this is too easy: even if men admit they are cowards, they still want to be saved. There is no "harmonious development," no child-rearing program, no self-reliance that would take away from men their need for a "beyond" on which to base the meaning of their lives. The fallacy of vulgar Marxism was that it overlooked the depth and universality of the fear of death; Marcuse has remedied this. The other fallacy was to fail to see the naturalness of existential guilt—and here Marcuse likewise fails. The task of social theory is to show how society aggravates and uses natural fears, but there is no way to get rid of the fears simply by showing how leaders use them or by saying that men must "take them in hand." Men will still take one another's heads *because their own heads stick out* and they feel exposed and guilty. The task of social theory is not to explain guilt away or to absorb it unthinkingly in still another destructive ideology, but to neutralize it and give it expression in truly creative and life-enhancing ideologies.

The question we are left with, then, is to whom does one expiate? So far as I can see, this is the dénouement of the Enlightenment quest for a science of society. It will be some combination of Marxist critical thought and a tragic dimension, a perspective on the inevitabilities of human unfreedom. In this, the science would share a place with historical religions: they are all critiques of false perceptions, of ignoble hero systems. A science of society, in other words, will be a study similar to the one envisaged by Old Testament prophets, Augustine, Kierkegaard, Max Scheler, William Hocking: it will be a critique of idolatry, of the costs of a too narrow focus for the dramatization of man's need for power and expiation.[24]

As Norman Brown so well summed it up in three brilliant pages, the prophetic function of religion is the same as the function of psychoanalysis: the "return of the repressed," the release from the unconscious of true perceptions of empirical reality in place of the wishful cultural and private fantasies we put there.[25] Both religion and psychoanalysis show man his basic creatureliness and attempt to pull the scales of his sublimations from his eyes. Both religion and psychoanalysis have discovered the same source of illusion: the fear of death which cripples life. Also religion has the same difficult mission as Freud: to overcome the fear of self-knowledge. Self-knowledge is the hardest human task because it risks revealing to the person how his self-esteem was built: on the powers of others in order to deny his own creatureliness and death. Character is the vital lie that covers over the painful ambiguities of man's worm-godlikeness—the despair of the human condition, the miraculousness of it tightly interwoven with the stink and decay of it. Religion as unrepression would reveal both truths about man: his wormlikeness as well as his godlikeness. Men deny both in order to live tranquilly in the world. Religion overcame this double denial by maintaining that for God everything is possible. What seems to man to be fixed and determined for all time, beyond human worm-like powers, is for God free and open, to do with what He will.

This gave the possibility of a new heroism, the heroism of sainthood. This meant living in primary awe at the miracle of the created object—including oneself in one's own godlikeness. Remember the awesome fascination of St. Francis with the revelations of the everyday world—a bird, a flower. It also meant unafraidness of one's own death, because of the incomparable majesty and power of God. And so religion overcomes the specific problems of fear-stricken animals, while at the same time showing them what empirical reality really is. *If* we were not fear-stricken animals who repressed awareness of ourselves and our world, *then* we would live in peace and unafraid of death, trusting to the Creator God and celebrating His creation. The ideal of religious sainthood, like that of psychoanalysis, is thus the opening up of perception: this is where religion and science meet.

But I am not saying that the science of society is merged into organized religion. Far from it. We know only too well how easily traditional religious heroism has given way to the hero systems of the secular societies. Today religionists wonder why youth has abandoned the churches, not wanting to realize that it is precisely because organized religion openly subscribes to a commercial-industrial hero system that is almost openly defunct; it so obviously denies reality, builds war machines against death, and banishes sacredness with bureaucratic dedication. Men are treated as things and the world is pulled down to their size. The churches subscribe to this empty heroics of possession, display, manipulation. I think that today Christianity is in trouble not because its myths are dead, but because it does not offer its ideal of heroic sainthood as an immediate personal one to be lived by all believers. In a perverse way, the churches have turned their backs both on the miraculousness of creation *and* on the need to do something heroic in this world. The early promise of Christianity was to bring about once and for all the social justice that the ancient world was crying for; Christianity never fulfilled this promise, and is as far away from it today as ever. No wonder it has trouble being taken seriously as a hero system.[26] Even worse, as they have done all through history the churches still bless unheroic wars and sanctify group hatred and victimage. It is an age-old story known to all, so there is no point in lingering on it. But these kinds of betrayal of an ideal heroism seem to be more and more obvious to today's youth. They are even becoming obvious to the organized religions themselves, which are wondering how to divorce themselves from defunct hero systems and recapture the imaginations and the heroic impulses that are stifled in the youth. One way, of course, is by a reaffirmation of traditional evangelism, which still seems to offer a way to overcome exaggerated fears of life and death by heroic dedication to special purity and worthiness. There is no easy way out of the dilemma, as Tillich and others have so well written; organized society seems to represent a necessary denial of religious heroism. In the United States today courageous priests like Daniel Berrigan are again proving this truth: that society will move against religious sainthood (heroism) when it poses a threat to its own system of heroic apotheosis, no matter how self-defeating and immoral that system has become.

Also, if we say that the science of society is partly immersed in a tragic perspective, this should not give any comfort to dogmatic conservatives. Man simply cannot accept human limitations as inevitable in the scheme of things. If we talk about the "Devil" side of human nature and about man's depravity, we cannot be fatalistic or cynical about them. If we are skeptical about utopia and acknowledge the Devil, it is only the better to fight for the angel side. Today there is a real onslaught of intellectual conservatism, recruiting some of our best thinkers and trying very adroitly to discredit leftist thought. It is all right to glorify thinkers like Edmund Burke and to offer profound theological and philosophical commentaries on the tragedies of the human condition, on the follies of history, on the natural limitations of man.[27] But this is not offered as a corrective, but as a substitute for social action, for the achievement of social justice, as an apologetic for the system as it is, for a traditional herd patriotism. This is what makes most "intellectual and moral conservatism" today fundamentally dishonest and hypocritical.

I agree that Marxism in its own dogmatic form has to be richly supplemented by a psychology that shows how men welcome unfreedom and how the basic motives of human nature remain unchanged. But I also know that differences in talent are not so biological or hereditary as conservatives often want to make out. Nor is freedom to obey and to delegate one's powers as free as they like to imagine. Sure, society goes on because of a silent accord by the majority that they prefer structure to chaos, and are willing to be lulled to sleep because of the security and ease it offers them. But it also holds over their heads the ideology of death, power, immortality—just as shamans and kings once did—and dominates them with it. The sophisticated Marxian question has to be asked in each society and in each epoch: how do we get rid of the power to mystify? The talents and the processes of mesmerization and mystification have to be exposed. Which is another way of saying that we have to work against both structural and psychological unfreedom in society. The task of science would be to expose both of these dimensions.

One of the reasons for our present disillusionment with theory in the social sciences is that it has done very little in this liberating direction. Even those intelligent social scientists who attempt a necessary balance between conservative and Marxist perspectives are amiss in this. If we read the last three pages of Gerhard Lenski's important book *Power and Privilege,* we get a vista of the future— but it is such a slow, patient, scientific future, still unrelated to the pressing problems of an insane world. All he seems to want to present us with is an indefinite program extending far into the un- known future, devoted to patient checking, refining, extending the blend of conservatism and Marxism. I am hardly saying that social theory should stop dead and not be perfected; what I am saying is that a general critical science of society that unites the best of both wings of thought is a *present* reality, and need not be delayed. We have, as of today, a powerful critique of hero systems, of systems of death denial and the toll that they take. It is a toll of un- fulfilled life based on a continuing denial of social justice; it is a toll of internal victimage based on the inequality of social classes and the state repression of freedom; it is a toll of external victimage that helps siphon off internal social discontent and transform magically social problems into military adventures. Whatever form of government uses victimage, the use is still the same: to purify evil social arrangements, distract attention from the failure to solve internal problems. Scientists must expose these things from their own scientific forums. In science, as in authentic religion, there is no easy refuge for empty-headed patriotism, or for putting off to some future date the exposure of large-scale social lies.

I don't see why conservatives and radicals could not unite on such a science, if their sentiments are where their words are. Both believe in free public information, increasing the awareness of the masses as well as their responsibility. Both wings of thought agree on limiting the authority of the leaders, exposing their talents for mesmerization and their shortcomings. This is, after all, the dearest and grandest feature of a democracy, that it tries to keep these critical functions alive. The problem has always been that the leader is the one who usually is the grandest patriot, which means the one who embraces the ongoing system of death denial with the heartiest hug, the hottest tears, and the least critical distance. As Zilboorg pointed out so penetratingly, the leader lives with his head full into the clouds of the cultural symbols; he lives in an abstract world, a world detached from concrete realities of hunger, suffering, death; his feet are off the ground, he carries out his duties much like funeral directors and men who perform autopsies or executions—in a kind of emotional and psychological divorce from the realities of what he is doing.[28] The result is that the leader is actually in a state of limited responsibility to human beings in this world—and what power he has in this state! The whole thing is lopsided and rather eerie—like compulsive neurosis or psychosis, says Zilboorg. Words, symbols, shadowboxing—no wonder so much pulsating life is so serenely ground up by the nation-states.

It is all too true, alas, but we do not live in an ideal world. If we wanted to imagine such a world, give in to utopian fantasies, we already know what we would want our leaders to be like: persons who abstracted and objected least, who took each single life and its suffering full in the face as it is. Which is another way of saying that they would know the reality of death as a primary problem. We might even let our musings go wild while we are at it, and imagine that we would choose leaders for exactly this quality: that they themselves were conscious of *their own* fear of life and death, and of the cultural system as a way of heroic transcendence—but a way that is not absolute, that is relative and not timeless. This might be another way of saying that we would want our leaders to be "well-analyzed" men, except that even the best analysis does not guarantee to produce this level of self-conscious, tragic sophistication.

Yet, democracy does encroach on utopia a little bit, because it already addresses itself to the problem of mystification by free flow of self-criticism. We could carry the utopian musings further and say that the gauge of a truly free society would be the extent to which it admitted its own central fear of death and questioned its own system of heroic transcendence—and this is precisely what democracy is doing much of the time. This is why authoritarians always scoff at it: it seems ridiculously intent on discrediting itself. The free flow of criticism, satire, art, and science is a continuous attack on the cultural fiction—which is why totalitarians from Plato to Mao have to control these things, as has long been known. If we look at the dénouement of psychiatry and social science today, they represent a fairly thorough self-revelation of the fictional nature of human meanings—and nothing is theoretically more powerfully liberating than that. Lifton has even detected self-mockery and caricature as peculiar signs of a new type of modern man who is attempting to transcend the horror and absurdity of his cultural world.[29]

Conclusion

If I wanted to give in weakly to the most utopian fantasy I know, it would be one that pictures a world-scientific body composed of leading minds in all fields, working under an agreed general theory of human unhappiness. They would reveal to mankind the reasons for its self-created unhappiness and self-induced defeat; they would explain how each society is a hero system which embodies in itself a dramatization of power and expiation; how this is at once its peculiar beauty and its destructive demonism; how men defeat themselves by trying to bring absolute purity and goodness into the world. They would argue and propagandize for the nonabsoluteness of the many different hero systems in the family of nations, and make public a continuing assessment of the costs of mankind's impossible aims and paradoxes: how a given society is trying too hard to get rid of guilt and the terror of death by laying its trip on a neighbor. Then men might struggle, even in anguish, to come to terms with themselves and their world.

Yet I know that this is a fantasy; I can imagine how popular and influential such a body would be on the planet; it would be the perfect scapegoat for all nations. And so, like a true Enlightenment dreamer, now supposedly sobered by experience, I turn my gaze to the stars and imagine how wiser visitors from some other planet would admire such a world-scientific body. But nothing, then, changes: must we scientists still despair of the masses of men and forever turn our yearnings to the Fredericks and the Catherines— but now in outer-space garb? Or perhaps, like the monks in Walter Miller's great science-fiction tale *A Canticle for Leibowitz,* we should rocket our carefully shepherded manuscripts from this planet to another; and when that one, too, falls into ashes for having ignored the wisdom about evil that we have so painfully compiled, rocket them still again to another world—a sort of eternal pilgrimage into space, looking for a place where men will finally take command of their drivenness.

Fortunately, no one mind can pose as an authority on the future; the manifold of events is so complex that it is fraud for the intellectual to want to be taken seriously as prophet, either in his fantasies or in his realities. One of the last thoughts of the great Williams James was that when all is said and done there is no advice to be given. And if a man of Freud's stature shrank back before prophecy, I surely am not going to peep any note of it at all. When we throw a wide net over the seething planet we have to admit that there is really nothing anyone can say about the possibilities for man; thinkers who have understood human nature and could take in the largest picture of history and tragedy have always shrunk back and shook their heads. Yet I think that there is a solid minimum achievement. If we can't go much beyond Freud's pessimism, at least we have subjected it to an empirical scientific statement—something that Freud did not satisfactorily do.

It seems to me that this leaves a margin for reason in the affairs of men. If men kill out of animal fears, then conceivably fears can always be examined and calmed; but if men kill out of lust, then butchery is a fatality for all time. The writer Elie Wiesel, who survived a Nazi concentration camp, summed it all up in a wistful remark during a TV interview: "Man is not human." But it is one thing to say that man is not human because he is a vicious animal, and another to say that it is because he is a frightened creature who tries to secure a victory over his limitations. Melville's moral in *Billy Budd* was that men need desperately to make panic look like reason. So it is the disguise of panic that makes men live in ugliness, and not the natural animal wallowing. It seems to me that this means that evil itself is now amenable to critical analysis and, conceivably, to the sway of reason. Freud speculated that it was possible that cultural developments might lie ahead which might make it possible even to renounce age-old instinctual satisfactions.[30] It is even easier to speculate about cultural developments that might influence the fear of death and the forms of heroism, and so blunt the terrible destructiveness that they have caused.

This is truly the great gain of post-Freudian thought; it gives us a merger of science and tragedy on a sophisticated level, one where science does not drop out of the picture. We surely will never be able to do great things with our condition on this planet, but we can again throw something solid into the balance of irrationalism. When all is said and done about the failure of thought to influence man's fate, we have already witnessed great things in our time: Marxism has already had an enormous influence for human survival: it stopped Hitler in Russia, and it eliminated the gratuitous and age-old miseries of the most numerous people on earth. We have no way of knowing what gain will come out of Freudian thought when it is finally assimilated in its tragic and true meanings. Perhaps it will introduce just that minute measure of reason to balance destruction.

References

Note: The works of A. M. Hocart and Otto Rank are mentioned frequently throughout, so that they have been abbreviated in the references as follows:

A. M. Hocart

SO *Social Origins* (London: Watts, 1954), foreword by Lord Raglan.
KC *Kings and Councillors*, 1936 (Chicago: University of Chicago Press, 1970), ed. Rodney Needham.
K   *Kingship*, 1927 (London: Oxford University Press, 1969).
PM *The Progress of Man* (London: Oxford University Press, 1933).
LGM *The Life-giving Myth* (London: Methuen, 1952), ed. Lord Raglan.

Otto Rank

PS *Psychology and the Soul*, 1931 (New York: Perpetua Books edition, 1961).
ME *Modern Education: A Critique of its Fundamental Ideas* (New York: Knopf, 1932).
WT *Will Therapy and Truth and Reality*, 1936 (New York: Knopf, 1945, one-volume edition).
BP *Beyond Psychology*, 1941 (New York: Dover Books, 1958).
AA *Art and Artist*, 1932 (New York: Agathon Press, 1968).

Norman O. Brown's frequently cited *Life against Death: The Psychoanalytical Meaning of History* (New York: Viking, 1959) is abbreviated as LAD.

Epigraph

1. William James, *The Varieties of Religious Experience* (New York: Mentor, 1958), pp. 137–138.

Introduction

1. Rank, PS, pp. 143–145.
2. Leo Tolstoy, *A Confession*, 1882 (London: Oxford University Press, 1961 edition), p. 24.
3. Rank, BP, p. 208.
4. *Ibid.*, p. 63.
5. Ernest Becker, *The Denial of Death* (New York: The Free Press, 1973).

Chapter One

1. Hocart, SO, p. 87.
2. Hocart, PM, p. 133.
3. Mircea Eliade, *Cosmos and History* (New York: Harper Torchbooks, 1959), pp. 44 ff.
4. Hocart, K, p. 201.
5. Claude Lévi-Strauss, *Structural Anthropology* (New York: Basic Books, 1963), pp. 132 ff., and *The Savage Mind* (London: Weidenfeld and Nicolson, 1966).
6. J. Huizinga, *Homo Ludens*, 1950 (Boston: Beacon Press, 1960), p. 53.
7. Hocart, KC, pp. 289–290.
8. *Ibid.*, pp. 37, 290.
9. James, *Varieties of Religious Experience*, p. 119.
10. Helmut Schoeck, *Envy: A Theory of Social Behavior*, 1969 (New York: Harcourt, Brace & World, 1970), p. 86.
11. Alan Harrington, *The Immortalist* (New York: Random House, 1969), p. 115.
12. Erving Goffman, *Interaction Ritual* (New York: Doubleday Anchor Books, 1967); *The Presentation of Self in Everyday Life* (New York: Doubleday Anchor Books, 1959).
13. Hocart, KC, pp. 285–286.
14. Robert Hertz, *Death and the Right Hand* (New York: The Free Press, 1960).
15. Hocart, K, p. 198.
16. Rank, AA; see especially chaps. 5–10. See also G. Van der Leeuw, *Religion in Essence and Manifestation* (New York: Harper Torchbooks, 1963), and Eliade, *Cosmos and History*.
17. Hocart, SO, pp. 92 ff.
18. *Ibid.*, p. 21; K, pp. 25, 152.
19. Hocart, K, pp. 190 ff.
20. *Ibid.*, pp. 199 ff.
21. *Ibid.*, pp. 201–202, 224.
22. Hocart, PM, p. 133.
23. Hocart, K, p. 243.
24. Lévi-Strauss, *The Savage Mind*.
25. Becker, *The Denial of Death*.

26. Hocart, KC, pp. 53–54.
27. Hocart, SO, p. 35.

Chapter Two

1. Brown, LAD.
2. Géza Róheim, *Psychoanalysis and Anthropology* (New York: International Universities Press, 1969).
3. Brown, LAD, p. 261.
4. Marcel Mauss, *The Gift* (Glencoe: The Free Press, 1954).
5. Brown, LAD, p. 271.
6. Van der Leeuw, *Religion*, vol. 2, chap. 50.
7. *Ibid.*, p. 356.
8. Hocart, LGM, pp. 102–103.
9. Géza Róheim, "The Evolution of Culture," *International Journal of Psychoanalysis*, 1934, 15:401.
10. Brown, LAD, p. 260.
11. *Ibid.*, p. 268.
12. *Ibid.*
13. Rank, WT, p. 87.
14. Cf. Paul Tillich's discussion of the "ambiguities of life" in *Systematic Theology* (Chicago: University of Chicago Press, 1963), vol. 3.
15. A. J. Levin, "The Fiction of the Death Instinct," *Psychiatric Quarterly*, 1951, 25:269.
16. Cf. H. H. Turney-High, *Primitive War: Its Practice and Concepts* (Columbia: University of South Carolina Press, 1971), pp. 196–204.
17. Levin, "The Fiction of the Death Instinct," p. 268, expanding an idea of J. C. Moloney's *The Magic Cloak* (Wakefield, Mass.: Montrose Press, 1949), p. 213.
18. Brown, LAD, pp. 265–266.
19. *Ibid.*, p. 280.
20. Cf. Van der Leeuw, *Religion*, vol. 2, pp. 463 ff.
21. *Ibid.*, pp. 468–469.

Chapter Three

1. Brown, LAD, p. 252.
2. Claude Lévi-Strauss, *A World on the Wane* (London: Hutchinson & Co., 1961).

3. Jean-Jacques Rousseau, *The First and Second Discourses,* 1755 (New York: St. Martin's, 1964), ed. R. D. Masters.

4. Brown, LAD, p. 242.

5. Rousseau, *The First and Second Discourses,* p. 141.

6. *Ibid.,* p. 174.

7. *Ibid.,* p. 149.

8. W. C. Lehman, *Adam Ferguson and the Beginnings of Modern Sociology* (New York: Columbia University Press, 1930), pp. 82 ff.

9. G. Landtmann, *Origin of the Inequality of the Social Classes* (Chicago: University of Chicago Press, 1938), chap. 3.

10. *Ibid.,* p. 54.

11. *Ibid.,* pp. 55 ff.

12. Morton H. Fried, *The Evolution of Political Society* (New York: Random House, 1967), especially pp. 182 ff.

13. Rank, ME, p. 13.

14. Rank, BP, p. 103.

15. Robert H. Lowie, *Lowie's Selected Papers in Anthropology* (Berkeley: University of California Press, 1960), in Cora Du Bois, ed., pp. 279 ff.

16. Thomas Hobbes, *The Leviathan,* 1651 (New York: Liberal Arts, 1958), chap. 11.

17. Cf. M. Eliade, *Shamanism: Archaic Techniques of Ecstasy* (New York: Pantheon, 1964).

18. P. Radin, *The World of Primitive Man* (New York: Grove Press, 1960), p. 140.

19. *Ibid.,* chap. 7.

20. *Ibid.*

21. Lehman, *Adam Ferguson and the Beginnings of Modern Sociology,* pp. 113 ff.

22. Brown, LAD, pp. 251–252.

23. *Ibid.,* p. 252.

24. G. Lenski, *Power and Privilege* (New York: McGraw-Hill, 1966), p. 105.

Chapter Four

1. Radin, *The World of Primitive Man,* pp. 213 ff.

2. Fried, *The Evolution of Political Society,* pp. 117–118.

3. Hocart, KC, p. 138.

4. *Ibid.*, p. 134.

5. *Ibid.*, pp. 134, 206.

6. Hocart, K, p. 209.

7. *Ibid.*, p. 41.

8. *Ibid.*, p. 45.

9. Henri Frankfort, *Ancient Egyptian Religion* (New York: Harper Torchbooks, 1961), pp. 56–57.

10. Hocart, KC, p. 203.

11. *Ibid.*, p. 154.

12. *Ibid.*, p. 139.

13. *Ibid.*, p. 153.

14. Robert H. Lowie, "Some Aspects of Political Organization among the American Aborigines," in Cora Du Bois, ed., *Lowie's Selected Papers in Anthropology* (Berkeley: University of California Press, 1960), chap. 21; Radin, *The World of Primitive Man*, pp. 214–215.

15. Fried, *The Evolution of Political Society*, p. 180.

16. Cf. Róheim, "The Evolution of Culture," p. 402.

17. Hocart, PM, p. 237.

Chapter Five

1. Karl Lamprecht, *What Is History?* (New York: Macmillan, 1905), p. 29.

2. Rank, PS, p. 87.

3. Brown, LAD, p. 285.

4. Rank, PS, p. 18.

5. *Ibid.*, p. 38; cf. Emile Durkheim, *Incest: The Nature and Origin of the Taboo*, 1897 (New York: Lyle Stuart, 1963), p. 109.

6. Cf. F. M. Cornford, *From Religion to Philosophy*, 1912 (New York: Harper Torchbooks, 1957), p. 109.

7. Rank, BP, p. 126.

8. *Ibid.*, p. 125.

9. A. Moret and G. Davy, *From Clan to Empire* (New York: Knopf, 1926), p. 360.

10. Cf. "Religion, Magic and Morale," in Douglas G. Haring, ed., *Japan's Prospect* (Cambridge, Mass.: Harvard University Press, 1946), chap. 7.

11. Rank, BP, pp. 162 ff.

12. *Ibid.*, p. 135.
13. *Ibid.*, p. 128.
14. *Ibid.*, p. 127.
15. *Ibid.*, p. 128.

Chapter Six

1. Brown, LAD, pp. 127–128.
2. *Ibid.*, p. 248.
3. *Ibid.*, p. 283.
4. *Ibid.*, p. 286.
5. *Ibid.*, pp. 279, 281, 283.
6. Mary Douglas, *Purity and Danger: An Analysis of Concepts of Pollution and Taboo* (British Penguin Books, 1966), pp. 85–86.
7. Brown, LAD, p. 247.
8. Cf. Landtmann, *Origin of the Inequality of the Social Classes*, pp. 60–61.
9. G. E. Smith, *Human History* (New York, 1929), as quoted in S. A. Coblentz, *Avarice: A History* (Washington: Public Affairs Press, 1965), p. 24.
10. Hocart, LGM, p. 99.
11. Brown, LAD, p. 247.
12. Hocart, LGM, p. 101.
13. Róheim, "The Evolution of Culture," p. 402.
14. Hocart, LGM, p. 103.
15. O. Spengler, *The Decline of the West* (New York: Knopf, 1939, one-volume edition), p. 489.
16. Brown, LAD, pp. 246, 248.
17. *Ibid.*, p. 251.
18. *Ibid.*, p. 295.
19. *Ibid.*, pp. 289–293.
20. P. Tempels, *Bantu Philosophy* (Paris: Presence Africaine, 1959), p. 118.
21. Rank, BP, p. 128.
22. Brown, LAD, p. 215.
23. On the symbolic role of money in recent American life, see Hugh Duncan's excellent little chapter "Money as a Form of Transcendence

in American Life," in his *Communication and Social Order* (New York: Bedminster Press, 1962), chap. 26.

24. *Ibid.*, p. 278.
25. *Ibid.*, p. 279.
26. G. Heard, *The Ascent of Humanity: An Essay on the Evolution of Civilization from Group Consciousness through Individuality to Super-Consciousness* (London: Jonathan Cape, 1929), p. 71, note 5.
27. Brown, LAD, p. 272.
28. *Ibid.*, pp. 280, 283.

Chapter Seven

1. Rank, BP, pp. 58–59.
2. Wilhelm Reich, *The Mass Psychology of Fascism*, 1933 (New York: Farrar, Straus, 1970), pp. 334 ff.
3. *Ibid.*, p. 339.
4. Erich Neumann, *Depth Psychology and a New Ethic* (London: Hodder & Stoughton, 1969), p. 40.
5. Carl Jung, "After the Catastrophe," *Collected Works*, vol. 10 (Princeton, N.J.: Bollingen, 1970), p. 203.
6. *Ibid.*
7. Neumann, *Depth Psychology and a New Ethic*, p. 50.
8. Jung, "After the Catastrophe," p. 216.

Chapter Eight

1. Elias Canetti, *Crowds and Power* (London: Gollancz, 1962), p. 448.
2. J. J. Rousseau, "Discourse on the Origin and Foundations of Inequality among Men," in *The First and Second Discourses*, 1755 (New York: St. Martin's, 1964), ed. R. D. Masters, p. 161.
3. Lewis Mumford, *The Myth of the Machine: Technics and Human Development* (New York: Harcourt, Brace & World, 1966).
4. *Ibid.*, p. 226.
5. *Ibid.*, pp. 220–221.
6. *Ibid.*, pp. 58, 116, 218, 226 ff.
7. *Ibid.*, pp. 149–150, 308.
8. Cf., for example, Georges Gusdorf, *L'Expérience humaine du sacrifice* (Paris: Presses Universitaires de France, 1948); Louis Bouyer,

178   REFERENCES

Rite and Man: Natural Sacredness and Christian Liturgy (Notre Dame, Ind.: University of Notre Dame Press, 1963); H. Hubert and M. Mauss, *Sacrifice: Its Nature and Function*, 1898 (Chicago: University of Chicago Press, 1964); Van der Leeuw, *Religion*, vol. 2, chap. 50.

9. Mumford, *The Myth of the Machine*, pp. 185–186.
10. See H. Marcuse, "The Ideology of Death, in H. Feifel, ed., *The Meaning of Death* (New York: McGraw-Hill, 1965), p. 75, for a similar, powerful observation.
11. This is from Hubert and Mauss, *Sacrifice*, and Van der Leeuw, *Religion*, vol. 2, p. 356.
12. Leo Alexander, "Sociopsychologic Structure of the SS," *Archives of Neurology and Psychiatry*, 1948, 59:626.
13. Cf. Turney-High, *Primitive War*, pp. 189 ff. This is at odds with Mumford's hypothesis in *Myth of the Machine*, p. 218.
14. Cf. Canetti, *Crowds and Power*, pp. 139–140.
15. J. Huizinga, *Homo Ludens* (Boston: Beacon Press, 1955), p. 91.
16. Canetti, *Crowds and Power*, p. 228.
17. *Ibid.*, p. 230.
18. Cf. G. Landtmann, *Origin of the Inequality of Social Classes*, pp. 42 ff.
19. *Vancouver Sun*, British Columbia, Canada, Oct. 15, 1971.
20. Rank, WT, p. 130.
21. Freud, "Thought for the Times on War and Death" and "Why War?" *Collected Papers*, 1932 (New York: Basic Books, 1959), vols. 4 and 5.
22. Freud, "Thought for the Times on War and Death," vol. 4, p. 314.
23. Harrington, *The Immortalist*, p. 49.
24. Cf. Canetti's interesting insight on Domitian's way of experiencing the very *process* of survival in *Crowds and Power*, p. 234.
25. *Ibid.*, pp. 138–140.
26. Rank, PS, pp. 73–74; my emphasis.
27. J. Scher, "Death: The Giver of Life," in H. M. Ruitenbeek, ed., *Death: Interpretations* (New York: Delta Books, 1969), pp. 103–104.
28. G. Zilboorg, "Fear of Death," *Psychoanalytic Quarterly*, 1943, 12:472.
29. Rank, BP, pp. 40–41.

30. Harrington, *The Immortalist,* pp. 138–139.

31. Zilboorg, "Fear of Death," pp. 473–474.

32. In H. D. Duncan, *Communication and Social Order* (New York: Bedminster Press, 1962), p. 127.

33. H. D. Duncan, *Symbols in Society* (New York: Oxford University Press, 1968), p. 242; also, *Symbols and Social Theory* (New York: Oxford University Press, 1969), pp. 266–267.

34. Duncan, *Communication and Social Order,* p. 131.

35. Quoted in H. Feifel, ed., *The Meaning of Death* (New York: McGraw-Hill, 1965), p. 62.

36. Rank, BP, pp. 168–169.

37. Quoted in Brown, LAD, p. 10.

38. Duncan, *Communication and Social Order,* p. 132.

39. Duncan, *Symbols in Society,* p. 39.

40. *Ibid.,* pp. 39–40.

41. Cf. Kenneth Burke, "The Rhetoric of Hitler's 'Battle,'" *The Philosophy of Literary Form* (New York: Vintage Books, 1957). Cf. also Duncan, *Communication and Social Order,* especially chaps. 17 and 18, and *Symbols in Society,* chap. 4.

42. Cf. A. Koestler, *Darkness at Noon,* and Duncan, *Symbols and Social Theory,* bibliography on p. 304.

43. Kenneth Burke, in Duncan, *Symbols and Social Theory,* p. 269; Duncan, *Communication and Social Order,* p. 127.

44. R. J. Lifton, *Revolutionary Immortality: Mao Tse-tung and the Chinese Cultural Revolution* (New York: Vintage Books, 1968), p. 40.

45. *Ibid.,* p. 81.

46. *Ibid.,* pp. 68 ff.

47. Cf. Rank, BP, pp. 40–41.

48. Lifton, *Revolutionary Immortality,* pp. 7–8.

49. Harrington, *The Immortalist,* p. 131.

50. Cf. Brown's synthesis, LAD, chap. 14.

51. Lifton, *Revolutionary Immortality,* p. 25.

52. *Ibid.,* p. 84.

53. Duncan, *Symbols in Society,* chap. 4; *Symbols and Social Theory,* chap. 23.

54. Harrington, *The Immortalist*, p. 64.

55. Cf. E. Becker, *Beyond Alienation* (New York: Braziller, 1967), pp. 182–195.

56. Cf. J. C. Moloney, *The Magic Cloak* (Wakefield: Montrose Press, 1949); Levin, "The Fiction of the Death Instinct"; Marcuse, "The Ideology of Death."

Chapter Nine

1. Rousseau, *The First and Second Discourses*, p. 129.

2. *Ibid.*, p. 149.

3. *Ibid.*, pp. 179–180.

4. *Ibid.*, pp. 151, 179.

5. James Frazer, *The New Golden Bough*, 1890 (New York: Criterion Books, 1959, abridged one-volume edition), ed. T. H. Gaster, pp. 54–60, 223 ff.

6. G. Heard, *The Ascent of Humanity*, pp. 68 ff.

7. E. Canetti, *Crowds and Power*, pp. 225–278, 411–434.

8. A. Koestler, "The Urge to Self-destruction," in A. Tiselius and S. Nilsson, eds., *The Place of Value in a World of Facts: Proceedings of the Fourteenth Nobel Symposium* (New York: Wiley, 1970), pp. 301–304; also Koestler's *The Ghost in the Machine* (New York: Macmillan, 1967), chap. 15.

9. E. Becker, *The Birth and Death of Meaning* (New York: The Free Press, 1971 edition), p. 172.

10. Erich Fromm, *The Heart of Man: Its Genius for Good and Evil* (New York: Harper & Row, 1964).

11. See Julius Hecker, *Russian Sociology* (London: Chapman and Hall, 1934), pp. 119–120.

12. Quoted in Lifton, *Revolutionary Immortality*, epigraph.

13. See H. H. Turney-High, *Primitive War*, chaps. eight through ten. On unresolved grief as a motive for murder, see Ronald Kuhn's classic study, "The Attempted Murder of a Prostitute," in Rollo May et al., eds., *Existence: a New Dimension in Psychiatry and Psychology* (New York: Basic Books, 1958).

14. See Koestler, "Urge to Self-destruction," p. 302.

15. K. Lorenz, *On Aggression* (New York: Harcourt, Brace & World, 1966), p. 403.

16. Freud, *Group Psychology and the Analysis of the Ego* (New York: Bantam Books edition, 1965).
17. Koestler, *The Ghost in the Machine*, pp. 251–253.
18. *Ibid.*, p. 234.
19. Fromm, *The Heart of Man*, p. 56.
20. Lenski, *Power and Privilege*, pp. 441–443.
21. *Ibid.*, p. 105.
22. C. Kluckhohn, *Navaho Witchcraft* (Boston: Beacon Press, 1944), pp. 89, 95.
23. See John G. Kennedy, "Psychosocial Dynamics of Witchcraft Systems," *International Journal of Social Psychiatry*, 1969, 15:177; note also the convolutions on this problem from within psychoanalysis—from the Marxian Otto Fenichel to A. Mitscherlich, "Psychoanalysis and the Aggression of Large Groups," *International Journal of Psychoanalysis*, 1971, 52:161–167.
24. K. Burke, "The Rhetoric of Hitler's 'Battle,'" pp. 187–188.

Chapter Ten

1. P. Ricoeur, *Symbolism of Evil* (New York: Harper & Row, 1967), p. 351.
2. Cf. Charles H. Cook, Jr., "Ahab's 'Intolerable Allegory,'" *Boston University Studies in English*, 1955–1956, 1:45–52.
3. Freud, *Civilization and Its Discontents*, 1929 (London: Hogarth, 1969), p. 82.
4. Freud, *The Future of an Illusion*, 1927 (New York: Doubleday Anchor Books, 1964), p. 12.
5. Jung, *Transference* (Princeton, N.J.: Princeton University Press, 1969), p. 56.
6. Rank, ME, p. 200.
7. Freud, "Observations on Transference-Love," *Collected Papers*, 1915 (New York: Basic Books, 1959), vol. 2, p. 388.
8. Rank, BP, p. 272.
9. Rank, PS, p. 192.
10. Rank, BP, p. 273.
11. Cf. I. Progoff, *The Death and Rebirth of Psychology* (New York: Dell, 1956), p. 262.
12. Quoted in *ibid.*, p. 81.

13. Rank, WT, p. 253.
14. Jung, *Transference*, pp. 71–72.
15. Fromm, "The Social Philosophy of 'Will Therapy,'" *Psychiatry,* 1939, 2:229–237.
16. Cf. Rank's balanced view, BP, p. 15.
17. P. Pruyser, *A Dynamic Psychology of Religion* (New York: Harper & Row, 1968), p. 8.
18. This thesis has been worked on by several writers—most recently, I think, by Sidney Hook, *The Hero in History* (Boston: Beacon Press, 1955).
19. Julius Hecker, *Russian Sociology* (London: Chapman & Hall, 1934), pp. 119–120.
20. Marcuse, "The Ideology of Death," chap. 5.
21. *Ibid.,* p. 74.
22. Rank, ME, p. 232; my emphasis.
23. Marcuse, "The Ideology of Death," p. 72.
24. Cf. also Rank, WT, p. 62; Fromm, *Beyond the Chains of Illusion* (New York: Simon & Schuster, 1962), pp. 56 ff.; William F. Lynch, *Images of Hope* (New York: Omega Books, 1965).
25. Brown, LAD, pp. 231–233.
26. Cf. Rank, BP, p. 128.
27. See *The Intercollegiate Review: A Journal of Scholarship and Opinion.*
28. G. Zilboorg, "Authority and Leadership," *Bulletin of the World Federation of Mental Health,* 1950, 2:13–17.
29. Lifton, "Protean Man," *Partisan Review,* Winter, 1968, 13–27.
30. Freud, *The Future of an Illusion,* p. 13.

Index

Adler, Alfred, on neurosis as vanity, 158
Aggression:
  as a creative act, 155
  as heroic triumph over evil, 138–141
  and self-perpetuation, 107
Agriculture:
  and rise of patriarchal family, 66
  and rise of priests, 67
  (*See also* State)
Alexander, Leo, on SS and heathen concept, 103
Alice Cooper, 14
Anality, 32, 116
Arendt, Hannah, on Eichmann, 121–122, 134
Art and Artist (Rank), 60n.

Bantu, detribalization of, 83n.
Berrigan, Daniel, 164
Billy Budd (Melville), 169
Bridge on the River Kwai, The (film), 109
Brown, Norman O., 38, 40, 63, 73–76, 81
  economics as sacred, 28
  on guilt, 90
  money as denial of anality, 82
  psychoanalysis and religion, 163–164
  society as shared guilt, 32, 35–36
Buber, Martin, 138, 158
Buchenwald, as result of massive mystification, 117
Burke, Edmund, 128, 165
Burke, Kenneth, 118, 144–145
  civic enactment of redemption through victim, as universal motive, 114–115

Calvinism, compared with primitive religion, 31–32

Camus, Albert, 145
Canetti, Elias, 2, 96, 106n., 132
Cannibalism, 152
  as incorporation of spiritual and physical energy, 108
  Sergeant Danh Hun in Vietnam and, 108
Canticle for Leibowitz, A (Miller), 168
Causa sui project, 82, 88–89, 122–123, 125, 161
Child, alertness to power sources, 46
China, reliving idea of the primitive group soul, 119
Chinese Yin and Yang, 9
Christianity:
  crisis in, 164
  primitive, as threat to commercialism and communism, 86
  promise of universal democratic equality, 68–69, 86
  unfulfilled promise of, 70–72, 88, 164
Coins, sacred origins of, 79–80
Crucifixion, as *controlled* display of dying, 110
Culture:
  as antidote to terror, 92
  as immortality lie, 121
  religious nature of, 4
  as system of heroic death denial, 123–127

Darwinism, 142–143
Death:
  cultural transcendence over, 3
  fear of, exploited by establishments, 125–126
  primitive views of, 45
  repression of, 92
  (*See also* Human condition; Primitive world)
Democracy and utopia, 167

History:
as succession of immortality ideologies, 25, 64, 154
as testimonial to costs of heroism, 150
as tragic record of repressed guilt, 90
Hitler, 106
and idealism of German youth, 150
as a psychologist, 115–117, 142
Hobbes, Thomas:
on evil, 49
on power, 45
Hocart, A. M., 52–54, 62
money, 78
necessity of moiety for ritual, 11
primitive ritual as technique for controlling life, 6–8
prosperity as universal ambition, 2
Homo Ludens (Huizinga), 6
Hubris, 37, 59
Huizinga, 10
primitive life as playful dramatization, 15, 19
primitive war, 105
Human condition, 1–4
disease and death as principal evils of, 2–5, 148
heroism as transcendence over limitations of, 31
"instinct of self-preservation" as universal, 1–2, 148–149
paradox of, 3
religion and culture as what is most distinctive about, 3–4
and results of ethology, 1, 142*n*.
Human evil:
agreement between Freud, Rank, Reich, and Jung on causes of, 91–95
basic dynamic of, 91–95
heroic victory over, 124
Jung on, 95
Marxists versus conservatives on causes of, 133, 146–147
Mein Kampf (Hitler), 93
motivated by joys of heroism, 155
Neumann on Jung's symbolisms, 94–95
a psychology of, 135–145
Rank on, 91–92

Reich on, 92–94
and repressed guilt, 90
Human face, unique in nature, 34–35

Immortality power:
of accumulated wealth, 87
primitive modes of attaining, 6–25
new historical forms of, 63–66, 82
Immortality symbols, 65
Inequality:
Marxists versus conservatives on causes of, 128–129, 143–144
in primitive religion, 43–45
psychological dimensions of, 143
psychological motivations for, 40–51
(*See also* Evolution of inequality)
Ionesco, Eugene, 136

James, William, 12
heroism and evil, 149
Jeffersonian democracy:
failure of, 72
and Faustian man, 71–72
Jews:
imageless god of, 53
scapegoating of, 93, 123
Jung, Carl, 94–95, 158

Kennedy family as modern mana source, 55
King:
as centralizer of power and ritual, 56–57, 60
as a visible god, 53–55
Kingship (Hocart), 22
Kluckhohn, Clyde, aggressiveness, 144
Koestler, Arthur, on aggression, 134, 139–141
Kwakiutl potlatch, 59

Lamprecht, Karl, 62
Lévi-Strauss, Claude, 9–10, 19*n*., 23
Lifton, Robert J., on revolutionary immortality, 118–120, 123
Life against Death (Brown), 73
Lorenz, Konrad, aggression and mass enthusiasm, 138, 142
Lowie, Robert, 44, 58

Man:
basic historic periods of, 8
on cutting edge of evolution, 34